one
degree

one degree

A Story of How
Hope and Help Are Closer
Than You Think

BY PAUL WITTWER
with Bryan Norman

I would like to dedicate One Degree to the following, for they have all played a crucial role in my life.

To Ann Bellucci, for saving me from me.

To Dorney Thompson, for teaching me personal grace.

To Dr. Dennis Jenkins, DDS and the team at Designing Smiles in Sellersburg, Indiana, for my beautiful, restored smile and for friendship and personal support since 2000.

To Dave Carney, for his friendship and taking a business risk on me.

To Colonel Harland Sanders, for providing a road map for lifetime inspiration.

To Rhonda Lamothe, for becoming my guardian angel in some of my darkest hours.

To Dan Merrell, for lifting me up when I had doubts.

To Nigel Flack in London, England, for giving me the Internet domain 1degree.org even though we have never met or talked to one another. Thank you for believing in this mission.

To Walmart Greeters, for extending friendship and community across America

To Waffle House employees, for helping me share the love

To all of the doctors, nurses, and medical technicians, for keeping me alive.

To my psychiatrist, for helping me manage my challenges

To Mom and Dad, for nurturing my grit to survive, creative talents to thrive, and passion to serve others. No matter how challenging the circumstances, they always delivered sunshine to Billy and me.

To all of you, thanks for being my one degree of hope and help and more . . .

Table of Contents

Preface

Hi, my name is Paul."

Those five words have literally saved my life time and time again. And I believe they can save yours.

A friend of mine once told me, "Paul, I've never heard a story like yours. You've lived a remarkable life. It's truly one of the most gripping tales I've ever come across. You should share it."

I responded to him that indeed I have shared it with hundreds of people over the past few years, and that each time I did, something happened. Something unexpected.

Connection.

Those on the other end of my tale always listened with casual interest *until* they heard something that touched them deeply, intimately, personally. Without fail, they emotionally bonded with one or more of my triumphs or tragedies. I could see in their faces and hear in their tone of voice that memories had been triggered and emotions stirred.

And before I knew it, they were telling me their stories, pouring out details of their own existence, many unheard by anyone until they met me. We would cry, laugh, and share a hug. And we would leave the conversation changed people.

Changed because our lives had been impacted in a spiritual sense that goes way beyond human touch, raw emotion, or common experience.

My life had not always been like this. In truth, mine was so far gone, so close to its uncelebrated end, yet I was pulled back into the beauty of living by the love and risk of one person at a time. After one encounter on the day I planned to commit suicide, I began to embrace and form in my mind the concept of *one degree*. It changed my life forever. It goes something like this.

"You Are Not Alone"

The planet may be big, the population may be overwhelming, and hope may be fleeting, but *you are not alone*. There is a single person within your sphere of influence today that can impact your life in a powerful way if you will risk connecting with them.

When we are honest with ourselves, we have to admit we all have issues. We all have baggage, and we've all been burned and lost our faith in humankind at one time or another. But I believe that hope and help are nearby, and they have taken the shape of a person. They are walking beside me, standing right behind or in front of me, sitting close by.

Their lives connect to mine in a miraculous, mysterious way that can only be described as *divine orchestration*.

"There Is Hope"

I don't believe in chance, or luck, or even karma.

I believe in people. And destiny.

When I contemplated suicide, someone made me feel loved, like life was worth living.

When I was broke and homeless, someone took a chance on me, believing I could be successful.

When I thought I was stupid, someone told me I was smart, and I had a future.

When I was in the hospital with life-threatening challenges, someone cared, and I got better.

When my challenges became more than I could face alone, someone listened, cared, and called me "friend."

Someone has always been there for me. And they will be there for you.

You may not know them. Yet.

"I Can Help"

I would be a liar if I didn't tell you that there have been those in my life who have hurt me deeply. I am not immune to pain, disillusionment, or despair. I am still in therapy. I still need help. I work hard every day to control my weight, my diet, my attitude, and my influence. It grinds me down at times and wears me out. But one thing keeps me going. It's simply this.

Somewhere out there is a person who needs my help or who can help me.

Whatever the need is, no matter how desperate or seemingly impossible, a meeting can take place that will make all the difference. I must do all in my power to not miss that opportunity.

So must you.

I am not naive. Yes, there are those among us who do not seek our good, who are not to be trusted. But I don't let damaged people erode my faith in the power of one degree.

In fact, they give me a greater sense of purpose and realization of just how urgent my mission is. I am just *one degree* away from giving and receiving hope and help, maybe even to them. And nothing on this earth is going to stand in the way of that happening.

The beautiful purpose of *one degree* is the most powerful truth I've gleaned from my time on this planet. It reminds me that we are all here for each other. We have the power and courage to change ourselves and others through connecting to one another.

Hope + Help + Courage = Change. That's the one degree formula. I'm living proof that it's true.

It seems impossible, but the story you are about to read is true. All this stuff happened. (I've changed some names to protect their identities, but other than that, this is a true tale stranger than fiction.)

My story is ongoing, of course, making the conclusion of this book problematic at best. I'm not done, and life is not done with me. I'd like to believe that this story actually ends with you and what you decide to do about *one degree*.

Will you join me in changing the world one connection at a time?

1

The Heirloom My
Father Left Me

August 21, 2001. I arose with a singular thought: it is time
I got reacquainted with the heirloom my father left me, a single-
barrel Remington shotgun he treasured and used so comfortably it was like an arm he couldn't surgically attach.

To hold that gun is to be instantly transported to childhood memories of Dad's proud return from the rabbit hunt,
bobbing with a slow walk and a simple man's prides. Holding
that cold steel, I reminisced about the dove hunts when Dad
would take me out. The wordless walks through the woods and
fields, the slow and sustained excitement of doing something
grown men do, of learning it. To Dad, a gun was not a thing of
sport. It was a tool that provided life for our family, countless
meals offered up by a man's drive to feed his own.

Dad had grown up in a family with six children on a farm
six miles from my childhood home. Fewer people today can
understand how satisfying it is to have a universe six miles
square. You really get to know the land, get rooted in the
people and rhythms of the seasons. I guess you could say
Dad had become the overseer of that six miles, that he had a

particular interest in its upkeep and productivity. Whatever would happen in those six miles became his family's circumstances. And to any good man, that is no small thing.

In August 1949 Dad was killing, scalding, and plucking chickens for my mom and her kitchen. Once you sever a chicken's head, you submerge its body in scalding water to loosen the feathers. They're easier to pluck that way.

Though I wasn't even born yet, something happened that August day that I would hear told and retold throughout my life. Dad had taken his rusty hatchet to a small clique of chickens. And as usual, he carried them to the scalding water, gave them a dunk or two, and walked off a pace to start cleaning them. My brother, four years old, was standing by the enormous kettle. It was boiling over an open fire like a wicked brew of malice that wafted over my family. For reasons unknown, Billy fell in.

His knees were dangling across one side of the rim and his arms across the other, the same way you take a lazy float in an inner tube. His screams said more than words, and with his back turned, my father spun around and came running, pulling him from the kettle. Dad set Billy down gingerly on the bacteria-filled dust and yelled for Mom to call the fire department and police.

For the life of me, I've tried to put myself in Dad's waiting, scanning our country road for any sign of stirred dust, flickering lights, sound, anything. All the while, a young boy, a son, moans and writhes, wriggling his way through an irreversible moment.

The police arrived as Mom and Dad loaded Billy into the

backseat of the family car. Mom was holding him under the armpits while Dad cut off his clothes. As they sped to the hospital, Billy spoke sheepishly.

"Mommy, where are we going?"

"To the hospital."

"But Mommy, I can't go. I am dirty."

Apparently, what works on the chicken feathers works on humans too. Billy's dead, scalded skin was falling from his body, draping from his joints, diving off muscle and bone. He was not expected to live. Second- and third-degree burns covered 85 percent of his four-year-old body. Those sorts of numbers don't yield a happy ending.

The curse of that cauldron—or whatever forced Billy in—didn't get the job done. His life was spared, and he eventually recovered. He always carried his scars, though, reminders of his time close to death. What would follow in the years ahead would make you think there were more devilish schemes at play, prolonged pains, lives so close to joy but not quite grasping it—loneliness, dissent, distrust, and discord. From the day Billy fell into the kettle, my family tree became driftwood, knotty and worn, dislodged and wandering to nowhere.

This is the story I came into, a story of driftwood and pain. When I arrived in this world, my stage was set for the same quiet epic we all live. A story to see if we beat the odds and undo the curse. A story to prove that we have the mettle to fight back the evil that wishes to overrun our world, starting with us.

—

Those first three years on Beechdale had all the makings of a brilliant childhood. Fields for roaming and devising all manner of imaginary wars, hide-and-seek, family dinners with endless piles of watermelon, farm animals. Any boy would be lucky to have as much opportunity for mischief and revelry as I did.

But the black fog amassing over my family would eventually cover it all. During my growing-up years, into adolescence, and even into adulthood, my family driftwood bobbed along on a path of hardship.

My dad's Remington would be waiting for me years from then. But before the heirloom would be necessary, I had some life to experience, some illnesses to form, some weight to gain. These hardships frame where I've been and what I'm still fighting to this day. Perhaps they are universal, my battles. It wouldn't surprise me if they are.

Not the Same Anymore

When you're a kid, you don't think about the family ledger or what it takes to build a decent life. You think Christmas presents are made in Santa's workshop. The supermarket is one big food fight, the produce man chucking big, beautiful apples into your roller basket, the butcher, steak. Cars' gas tanks are magically refilled.

So, when we moved in April 1955 from my childhood1930s frame and clapboard farm home on Beechdale, I thought it was a vacation, that we'd be going back. No, we had moved to a new, 940-square-foot brick ranch home with two bedrooms, one bath, kitchen, living room, and unfinished basement. I learned later in life that Dad had taken on a $3,150 mortgage that stretched the family budget. A child of the Great Depression, he was a blue-collar worker whose work ethic—more than his paycheck—was his dignity. He scraped enough together to buy a used truck with $300 cash because a man needs a truck. It was a 1951 Ford pickup, which has significance that you'll learn about later. But from then on, paychecks in our house had a short jaunt from hand to mouth for several years. Dad was a hard worker, though, truly a hard worker, and he didn't shirk or sulk. Instead, to balance his incessant worrying about money, he worked harder and longer.

Though he did achieve debt freedom in the future, the move from Beechdale to Kavanaugh Road changed my life. The atmosphere of joy was instantly replaced by anxiety. And when you add an extra mile to a young boy's romp, the distance feels oceanic. I no longer found myself on family doorsteps at dusk asking if the cousins could come out and play. Just a mile away, I found myself in a foreign land with new sounds, new smells, no familiar faces, and a strange buzz in the wind.

Billy seemed fine, oddly. But I, without the hug of the familiar, started to go inside myself more, to withdraw. I took long, pointless walks in the pastures busting dirt clods.

By the time I entered first grade, I wasn't too fond of other children or myself. I had gained a lot of weight after the move, enough to give me strangely large breasts, which never bodes well for a man at any stage of life. And with a first name like Leslie, everyone made quick work of mincing me. I'd like to think it was just my imagination, or even my low self-esteem. But a taunt is a taunt. And breasts are breasts.

The Prophecy of a Future

Elementary school was rotten. That's all I can say. By the time I made it to high school, I had never had a girlfriend. I struggled in all my classes. I was a loser. At least, by the world's standards I was. One of the first things you did upon entering my high school was participate in a battery of written and manual dexterity tests. I guess it was a chance for the school system to see how much they undercut your potential.

After the tests were graded several days later, four students at a time were called into the office of the guidance counselor. If many of my damaging experiences would be a cluster of bruises spread out over time, the day I stepped into the counselor's office would be a swift jab straight to the jaw. Followed by an uppercut. And possibly a kick in the groin. I was in the room with one boy and two girls. The counselor looked at the boy and said he could be a doctor, lawyer, or anything he wanted to be. His father was one of only two doctors in our town.

She then turned to me, her countenance shifting from a smile to a restrained grimace. She shuffled papers, buying time to craft her words. She looked me dead in the eye and said, "You could be an asparagus sorter or work in a Tinker Toy factory." In my memory, the counselor said this with a devilish, delighted look in her eye, my own personal witch with a poisoned apple.

I was stunned, confused, embarrassed.

I thought for a moment, resisting the feeling that a prophecy had just been spoken into my life, and asked, "Why would I want a job like that?" It was the best defense I could manage on the fly.

"Because it is something you can do," she replied. I could barely get out of my chair. I was crushed and humiliated. Even worse, I rolled over like a dog used to beatings and instantly believed she was right. Whatever hairlike strand of dignity I had in my life disappeared without so much as a eulogy, like a spiderweb put to fire. I looked at her words in my outstretched palm and put it over my heart, a badge of my identity stitched on tight, a pledge of allegiance to my mediocrity.

That night, my Mom had prepared creamed wild asparagus on thinly sliced toast, a seasonal delicacy in our house. I avoided the kitchen.

Reverse Polarity

I struggled through high school. To deal with my low self esteem and self-loathing, I became the class clown—an excuse for poor grades. I had few real friends and stayed constantly busy with jobs outside of class never having a girlfriend or attending a prom. The guidance counselor's words were my shadow. And if a stranger's words can do that, the words a father speaks to a son are sticky like molasses. They hit the ears and crawl down all over. So when my father said on our way to college enrollment, "Son, what you do in the next four years will determine the level you live on the rest of your life," I was jolted. I wanted to lean into my destiny to do Dad proud.

He said this on the way to the University of Kentucky, which, it turned out, did not have an Asparagus Sorter major with a minor in Tinker Toy development. I willed myself to trade that prophecy for the dreams my parents had for me, for their strong belief that I had a fire waiting inside me to burn. My Dad's words—a father's words—had just lit the fuse.

Like any kid heading out into the world, my parents gave me all sorts of guidance from their point of view. Vivid dreams of a lawyer-son litigating big cases in the county seat were pitched by my father like a man trying to convert a nonbeliever. My mother urged me to become a minister so that I could do the converting myself. But I was lost and wounded. Years of listlessness, no confidence, and damning declarations had become entrenched. My Achilles heel had been fully severed one small swipe at a time.

College was the same song as high school, second verse. My inability to develop relationships, my weight, and my stupidity emanated a reverse polarity to all the kids who were eager to be drawn in, who needed new friends to weather the drastic change into independence. After my freshman year, it was obvious that I wasn't pulling out of my nosedive despite whose words I wanted to believe, so I moved off campus. And

I stayed ultra busy. I always had a job, a built-in excuse to avoid people and a means to outfit myself with the all the accoutrements of hiding.

Finally, in my senior year, I picked my major. I was well on my way to receiving a Bachelor of General Studies Degree, which translates into "I couldn't afford to *not* make up my mind anymore." Though this degree would allow me to graduate with my friends, it was a worthless title for a worthless brain. The worthless brain graduated May 11, 1974.

The Winding Path to Somewhere

My postgraduation foray into the working world was as random as a pinball game. I started a commercial and industrial electronics systems company with three partners, all of whom had families and homes. With little capital and revenue, I lived in the back of the shop for nearly two years, sleeping on a mattress placed on the floor. I ate food prepared on a two-burner hot plate and showered in a portable Sears shower catching the run-off in a galvanized wash tub. When there was enough cash to make payroll, I was the last to be paid. One by one the partners with families left for real jobs and predictable income. The business closed in the spring of 1977, and as the last man standing, I was saddled with debts from it and another start-up business I entered into before graduating.

My businesses, though they didn't succeed, taught me a lot about equipment and system sales to financial institutions. With that knowledge, I moved to Evansville, Indiana, where I established another business as an independent manufacturer's representative. I sold a variety of equipment and systems to banks and savings and loans, including security systems, modular bank buildings, and even outdoor plastic and neon signs. I was very successful and by age twenty-seven had a six figure income. Unfortunately, my turbulent life was very unsettled, but I did gain a real sense of tenacity, of seeing a path to success. I just couldn't walk that path . . . yet.

I threw away my rep business in 1981 to move from Evansville to Houston, Texas, where I was appointed branch manager of an outdoor plastic and neon sign company based out of Corpus Christi. The company was undergoing a financial turnaround and reorganization after being purchased by two wealthy Texans who had no prior experience in the industry. I quickly set up a lean, mean selling machine in Houston, delivering proposals to prospective clients in two days while competitors took two weeks. The closing rate went from under 20 percent to over 90 percent. In less than six months, a failing branch had quintupled in sales.

Early into my new tenure as the head honcho of my branch, the sign company owners called to inform me that, as a new manager in their ranks, I was to undergo some psychological testing. "It's standard," they explained, "for every manager in the company." My heart hit the floor. I was certain any trained professional would be able to break through my cover like a bull charging a gauze barricade. *They're going to find out I'm stupid, screwed up. And then they're going to fire me.*

When Your Brain Feels Small

The psychological testing was tense and difficult. I expected the following week when the psychologist would walk me through the results to be my release date from the company. I tried everything I could to keep my mind off of my inevitable failure.

When the week passed, the psychologist walked through the door all warmth and professionalism. I knew it was his poker face. I could tell he'd practiced this sort of "let 'em down easy" approach before. To be honest, I was really quite appreciative. If I was going to be fired, at least let me keep my dignity. I started to ease up a little knowing this might be my most pleasant failure to date.

"How do you think you performed on the tests?" he asked.

I paused, trying to figure out how much to say. I mean, I didn't want to let go of the shred of hope that, perhaps, he had missed all my lesser qualities. So I started out easy, only slightly self-deprecating.

"Well, historically I haven't had the best math skills," I paused tentatively with a slight upward glance to see his reaction. Still the warmth and professionalism. *Okay*, I thought, *good sign.* "And I don't have the strongest reading skills. I've always had trouble focusing."

And thus the conversation continued with me making an airtight case for my stupidity.

When I had finished, Mr. Psychologist looked at me and said, "Paul who did this to you?"

"Umm, what do you mean?" I asked.

"Somewhere along the way," he began, "someone convinced you that you don't have any abilities. Do you have any idea how this has happened?"

I knew instantly. I could see my high school guidance counselor's face swirling in front of me, ghostly. I could hear her words, wispy, floating before me like a mumblings from a crystal ball.

"Paul?" I heard faintly while I swam in my own little world. Then again, this time a little more force. *"Paul?"*

I came to, still sitting in front of the psychologist. I'm certain the pain on my face was unmistakable. I couldn't speak another word. The psychologist hadn't blown my cover or reinforced the damaging lies of my youth. No, he did something much more painful. He went to the canker of my history and simply placed his finger on it. The past can be a white-hot pain.

I put my head on the table in front of him, ashamed.

"Paul, look at me," he said. My head was lead. "Paul, please look at me."

I slowly locked eyes with this man who had transported me to the cellar of my life's despair.

"I don't know what has happened to you in your past. But I have some good news for you."

I perked.

"Your test scores are telling a different story. You have placed within the top 2 percent of all Americans. I would estimate your IQ at 152 or more."

The psychologist was beaming. Now I know why he was

all warmth that day. He thought he would give me a good ego boost and have something strong to report to the company owners. Instead, he sent me a life raft.

All that night following, I floated through the possibility that I wasn't a destined loser. I lamented what could've been with my relationships, my weight, my performance in college had I only known that I wasn't born to build Tinker Toys. Was there a life being lived in a parallel universe by the Paul with a 152 IQ?

People often become what they're told. They live in the small-town lies, impossible black holes where no light can escape. I wanted to go find my guidance counselor and wave my newfound intelligence in her face. Truthfully, I wanted to punish her for the days and nights of self-doubt and years of wandering. I wished she were dead so I could spit on her gravestone.

Gold Rush

The sign company eventually went under due to some internal improprieties. Some ringer accountant given an executive position turned out to be an embezzler and wasn't too forthright in his reporting standards, and the government shut our doors. I drove to my office one day and was greeted by an industrial-grade padlock. It was one of the first sustained successes I had ever experienced, and it was instantly yanked away from me. I wasn't quite sure what to do next.

I returned to Kentucky to be close to my family and regroup.

The day I arrived I could see my five-year-old silhouette in the pasture skipping stones across the dust and talking to the wind. I paused before I entered the house and resolved that the Paul who walked through the door would not be the same Paul who walked out years ago. I resolved to deny the hometown voices that wait for you on the stoop ready to drag you into the past.

Rather than haphazardly fall into the next thing, I hired an industrial psychologist to help me find a new career track. Since my testing with the sign company, I felt like the scarecrow after seeing the wizard. I finally had a brain. The new doctor ran some tests, matched my skills with different professions, and helped me find some options. When I met with him to talk about my waiting life, he had two options that matched my skills and abilities.

"The first option," he said, "is remote viewing for the military." He looked up beaming and proud of such a rare recommendation. There was even a tinge of jealousy, I think.

"Um . . ." I paused, "what is remote viewing for the military?"

"They take people like you and put you in a room, describe a conflict or battle scene somewhere in the world," he said excitedly, "and ask you to foretell how it will play out." I looked at him like he was nuts.

"Option number two?" I asked quickly. The doctor paused and seemed a bit deflated.

"Really?"

"Yes, option number two. Please."

"You should also consider working in a think tank." I

looked at him, puzzled, and asked him to explain. Obviously, my 152 IQ hadn't quite sunk in to a real intelligence. I still had much to learn about how the world could benefit from my just-budding talents.

"They take people like you," he began, "put you in a room, and introduce you to different products, services, and business models. You sit there and figure out all of the potential and necessary changes." This guy sure seemed fond of putting me in an isolated room somewhere, somehow. Maybe he thought I was a tad crazy, and this was his way of putting me in a more casual straightjacket.

The options on the table left something to be desired. In addition to getting an outside opinion, I had been doing my own research. I told the psychologist I knew what I wanted to do.

"Investing," I said, looking him square in the eye.

"Investing?" trickled out of him.

"Yeah, investing. I think I could be a great stockbroker, and I've always wanted to learn about the stock market."

"Paul, I've got to be honest, I don't think investing is the right route for you."

On and on I listened to his laundry list of weak persuasions. They weren't actually weak, but I had already made up my mind. The moment I saw a profession purely about wealth, my soul sat up straight. *Yeah, let's take that one*, it would cheer. I didn't even consider that my motivations could be less than noble. I acquiesced to my blind desire without so much as a blink.

I soon became employed by an investment firm in January

1983, took whatever tests made me legal, and I waded through my new, complicated world. The industrial psychologist was right, the retail brokerage environment was all wrong for me. I was a very aggressive marketer, sending out thousands of mailings to attract prospective clients. I hired a team of seminary students to make follow-up calls at night. I even produced and appeared in my own television commercials for my seminars (the scripts had to be approved by the Securities and Exchange Commission)—one of the first brokers in the United States to do so. While I quickly became a top producer, I reinvested all of my earnings back into the business. I also made risky investments with my own money that the firm identified, but I ended up losing tens of thousands of dollars. Through all that very soon I learned that what appealed to me most was finding a business looking to expand through buying other companies. Mergers and acquisitions (M&A), it's called.

I quickly left the traditional brokerage route and decided to start my own M&A firm September 14, 1984. Mind you, I had little, knew little. But I believed in myself. I found my first mergers and acquisitions client who wanted to buy a particular business in an industry in which he had experience. I wouldn't describe this guy as a sure bet. During one of our early meetings, he looked at his empty balance sheets, my empty experience, and he asked how I expected to survive in this new career and business. I paused, made disturbingly long eye contact and said, "Innate ability." It was the first time in my life I believed I was capable. The curse of my childhood was coming undone.

My personal start-up investment was $114 and some borrowed office furniture. I closed my first deal eight months later and nearly starved to death in the process!

The Heart Beating

If my brain and my self-esteem were growing in leaps and bounds, my physical heart failed to take their cues. I don't know why some people are born under a blessed star, and others wriggle from underneath a cursed rock. Me and my ancestry, we're the latter, a breed full of genetic diseases with a penchant for emotional imbalances, the kind that need medicine. The most notable is the family heart. It's a weak thing that untangles and spurts, a factory defect that made it past the inspectors. That organ multiplied in my parents and brother would bring great heartache, something that I've always referred to in my own mind as the "family badge," a heart bypass surgery scar that would eventually find its way to my dad's, mom's, and brother's chests. The look of that scar tissue, all shiny, leathery, and embossed, would bring so much dread throughout my life.

Billy

Now, if you recall, our story began with Billy dangling over a boiling cauldron. Billy was the classic older brother: confident, bullheaded, captain of our imaginary spaceship, chooser of his seat at the kitchen table, headlock giver, toy breaker. Like all little brothers would, I adored him.

Billy was a gifted student. Annoyingly gifted, really, because he could do anything he put his mind to. And I don't mean that in the way parents pump us up, the future presidents and astronauts of the world. Billy breezed through high school and graduated with honors. He did the same in college earning a chemical engineering degree. He could enter any profession where the phrase "it's not rocket science" wouldn't apply. After college he received his draft notice and elected to join the Navy, flying through Officer Candidate School to become a lieutenant junior grade on a nuclear submarine.

Growing up and living in his shadow, I marveled that he could do so much, be so much. After his service in the Navy, Billy returned to the University of Kentucky to become a dentist. With no prerequisite courses and a chemical engineering degree, he caught up quickly and became one of the oldest students ever accepted at that time. After graduation, he settled in a small town with his family and built a great dental practice. It seemed that his driftwood planted and slowly shot out roots of stability and security.

In the coming years, though, the family's genetic predispositions would catch up with Billy. He would get divorced. Mental illnesses slipped quietly into his bedsheets, bedfellows whispering incantations and turning dreams into nightmares. At age thirty-nine, Billy was admitted to a psychiatric ward in 1984 for a week and began a steady diet of lithium to manage his bipolar disorder. He had heart surgery two years later. His mental illness and open-heart surgery were traumatic events that changed the course of his life. At age fifty-two he had a second heart bypass surgery. Because he was divorced at the time of the second surgery, I was the closest relative who could care for him afterward out of the hospital. The doctors had to withhold his mental health medicines to perform the operation. Without them, within two days of the surgery, he completely unraveled. My childhood hero had become absolutely loony. It was too much to handle—as close to a living hell as I can remember—but I tried because that's what family does.

At three in the morning on the third day of recovery at my home, he declared that he wanted to be taken home immediately, sixty miles away in the middle of a raging thunderstorm. I loaded this bandaged mess gingerly into the passenger seat and drove through bolts of lightning with the windshield wipers frantically clearing our path. I deposited my unraveled brother at his house. On the drive back, both relieved and unbelievably sad for the empty passenger seat and all it meant, I blasted God for all of the ugly, poor health bestowed upon my family.

Mom

In 1963 my mother turned forty. She had torrents of emotions, Niagara-sized plummets of screaming and weeping and sweating. It was never diagnosed, but the closest thing my Dad could reference to explain it to me was that she had menopause. To a youngster, she was bedeviled, maniacal, tyrannical—not the Mom I knew. It was the only time in my life I stayed out of the kitchen when I was told.

Her tirades were on-again-off-again for two years. And then, one day, like a new next-door neighbor, a symptom appeared. My mother's gums started bleeding. It was quickly determined that she had Type 1 diabetes. I loved my mother, truly and deeply. Which is why it's so alien to see your greatest source of love and encouragement transform before your very eyes. Imagine a woman with a rolling pin, teeth pink, house shoes, and a wild look in her eyes that said, "Come near me and you shall know my wrath." My mother was a kind-hearted, heartwarming, hospitable, loving woman. But she was overtaken by the war swimming inside her.

In the coming years, Mom's troubles would come in and out of our lives like a deep space comet. From a heart attack at forty-four, to a heart bypass at fifty-two, to living nearly two decades with 21 percent heart capacity and Type I diabetes, to falling down the stairs and waking with seven broken ribs, to gall bladder surgery, to two years in a neck brace after a car accident . . . Mom, it seemed, was born with a sordid lottery. The only thing she could win was more trouble.

Still, it is one of my great prides that no matter how far she was knocked down, she always got up and did her best to make a good life in the midst of her troubles. For instance, when she was diagnosed with diabetes she lost fifty pounds and kept it off until the day she died. Her perseverance and unwillingness to lie down in her troubles have always been a source of hope and inspiration for me, as I've dealt with many of the things I witnessed growing up.

Dad

To a boy a basement is a glorious thing, a playground leagues below the earth full of ancient trinkets, bothersome cobwebs, and secrets to be discovered. Which is why it's a strange thing to hear your mother yelling for you. And not the "supper's ready" yell, but the frantic one, the one that injects ice into your veins. When I heard her yell, I rushed for the stairs, my mind racing. *I'm in trouble*, I thought. Midstride it came to me, *Then why am I running so fast to get to my punishment?* But any kid knows, you don't defy your mother, especially one who just yelled liked that.

I hit the top of the basement stairs and hooked the door frame with my hand to swing my charging momentum. I scuffed linoleum. I leapt over chairs left out from the table. And when I hit the living room, there it was. There he was. My Dad, back against the floor, arms and legs spread out, a skydiver who didn't pull the chute in time.

Dad was forty-seven, and he just had a heart attack. It was a snowy day.

My mother was a hot mess. She was darting everywhere trying to keep Dad comfortable until the ambulance arrived. She was at his side, talking to him sweetly, encouraging him. And her eyes ventured toward the kitchen in the direction where I was standing, and we locked eyes momentarily. Her face turned to pure sympathy, and I didn't understand why. I didn't understand why she should feel sorry for me when it was *Dad* who had just received a heart beating. Now I understand it, that I was witnessing my own future, and my mother knew it too.

The ambulance backed up across the front yard, every now and then its wheels spinning in the ice sheet that had frozen underneath a layer of powdery snow. It was a cold, cold day in my life that day December 2, 1967.

The ambulance tracks in the yard stayed put for a full three months until spring brought its sunshine eraser. That was about the same time my father came home from the hospital, when the tracks disappeared. He would never be fully healthy again, and my parents would never know a normal life again.

In 1977, Dad had his second heart attack and quickly earned his third in 1980. That third heart attack, we were told, was a grave situation. He had two choices: bypass surgery or death. To most, that would be an easy choice.

The Tributaries Combine

My father, twisted in knots and terminally ill with congestive heart failure, decided enough was enough. He was a simple man who planned everything, and he thought dying on Thursday would be best so he could be buried on a Sunday. The last day I saw him alive he looked at me and said, "I have enough money to do what I want, but I don't have my health. Go enjoy your life."

He got up from his rocking chair and walked three steps to the bed.

He looked back at me, "Son, there are a lot of things worse than death. I love you."

Dad died on August 13, 1987. While my mother was at her longstanding hair appointment, Dad, barely able to walk, got out the heirloom Remington and walked into the backyard. With the barrel placed to his chest he bent over and pulled the trigger. A neighbor two doors down heard the blast and saw him fall, lifeless. He was sixty-seven.

Sixteen months later, Mom would sit down on the sofa in the basement after waxing part of the floor by hand and would never get up. She was sixty-five.

———

It is impossible to describe what loneliness feels like, or depression, because those things are defined by absence, even an absence of words to define them. By the time I was thirty-six, I had lost the only two people in my life who ever believed in me, who ever loved me without condition. That and my brother was a mere fraction of what he used to be. I was so very alone, a deep space comet without an orbit.

August 7 of 2001, I was morbidly obese and diagnosed with Type II diabetes by my endocrinologist, Dr. Wood. With all the congenital heart diseases and emotional imbalances in my family, it felt like a long fuse had been lit on my life. I could see it trail out through the landscape until it disappeared over the horizon. But I knew it was coming, my genetics, my fuse.

Seven Pounds of Dust

August 21, 2001, where our story began. I approach my closet with reverence, reach to the rear, and find the stock of my father's Remington. *It's time to end it,* I think. A childhood and adolescence of confusion and pain can all be erased. A certain future of physical maladies can be avoided. *It is time*, I think, *to torch the driftwood.*

The cold steel is unmistakable. Pulling the barrel forward and looking straight into it, I think about the power of the blast, how a split second of fire and heat will blaze a path right through me, how it blew through my father. No more sorrow, no more badges, no more cauldrons. No more loneliness, no more failures. No strivings, confusion, uncertainty, asparagus.

I have the heirloom in my hand along with my father's suicide note that I've kept for years. It reads, "I can't stand the pain any longer. Please forgive me. I love you all very much." *There's one difference between you and me, Dad*, I think. *I don't have to ask forgiveness from anyone. There's no one left.*

The end will be sweet aspirin relief.

I mindlessly move my hand down the barrel and familiarize myself with the trigger. There's a strange feeling like my Dad is there, like I conjured him and two sets of hands are holding the gun. I feel strangely comforted, and his hand is over mine guiding it. My soul bows its head, and I know it is time.

Did I turn off the stove? Yes. The hand is clutching the gun like during the rabbit hunts.

The house is ready to be sold. The gun turns to face its holder.

The trigger finger slowly begins to pull.

The wallpaper! I didn't fix the wallpaper!

The trigger clicks and like a tiny big bang, lead spreads through a new universe where one man is gone. Where my dad is gone. I sit there, sad that I will never see him again. I sit there knowing I can't go until I fix the wallpaper.

2

Saved by Ann
and Wallpaper

It's strange how many numbers are involved when you want to
die. Time extends out past the horizon, a drunk line of sloppy
dominoes. Your meals become a countdown. Everything is
excruciatingly slow. You approach your life with a sort of
mechanical detachedness. When I was winding things down, I
became something like a certified accountant, trying to balance
the checkbook of my life, reviewing my life insurance, my bank
account, making sure everything was in order.

All was well except the wallpaper. See, my obsessive-
compulsive disorder (OCD) wouldn't allow me to leave until
the wallpaper was perfect. One of the illnesses that compelled my decision to commit suicide actually played the part
of savior too.

The person I had called to come fix it, Ann Bellucci, couldn't
be there for one week. I had to do something to fill the time,
so I made a phone call. "Hello, yes. I have a question for you.
What time do you open in the morning? . . . Okay great. I'll see
you then."

I was going on a field trip.

The Crematorium

The week between my first attempt at suicide and my upcoming suicide was actually quite useful. I had left a couple stones unturned in the preparations for my burial. I wanted to meet with a funeral director to finalize a few details. This was a matter-of-fact mission. If you can imagine the oddity of it, I spoke to the man who would likely hold the urn of my dusty remains like I was going to buy a vacuum from him.

He explained the process of cremation and burial and what would be needed as we sauntered through his showroom of caskets and urns. "This one is solid pewter," he said pointing to an urn as we strolled, "a very popular model. And this one is brass-plated, galvanized steel" as he waved his hand in a showcase style. "It's guaranteed not to rust. Guaranteed!" he enthusiastically reprised. I wondered why the industry of death is so concerned for the attributes of its products. I guess it's for those who remain.

My parents had purchased two cemetery plots beside them and given them to me. But I wanted the cheapest option, a package that would include: body pickup and transport direct to the crematorium; no memorial service; ashes stored in a simple, unadorned urn; a small vault on the grave site; and a nondescript headstone. I would be seven pounds of dust.

Saved by Paper

Ann, the gal who would come to fix my wallpaper, had been doing this sort of work for me for nearly ten years. We initially met through a decorator I knew and had hired to help me furnish my home. Ann and I were only acquaintances, but I would wager I was one of her most frequent customers. Every time she would visit the house, we'd have more conversation, learn a bit more about one another. We weren't close friends by any stretch, but we were congenial toward one another.

There were problems with a couple of seams in the bathroom and some edges that were peeling. I couldn't go shoot myself until that mess was fixed, couldn't bear the thought of my house being liquidated and someone seeing the bathroom wallpaper in that condition.

When Ann finally arrived, she came up the sidewalk overflowing with buckets, sponges, and a ladder. She had such a genuine smile. Her face is a rare one, with relaxed lines around the eyes and an expression of honesty. To look at her you would think she never told a lie.

My world had gotten to the point that the only people who came in my home were people who worked on it. While Ann was setting up her work, I was undergoing mine. She was prepping the bathroom, and I was sitting down to type my suicide note. Today would be the day—it would time out perfectly. She would straighten the seams, and I would straighten on the grass in the backyard.

As I'm sure you can imagine, I wasn't perky and giggly. I was single-finger pecking at the keyboard and crying my eyes out. I had been saving these emotions from the week before, steadying myself until I knew they could climax. I think Ann must have heard me because she walked in my office and asked what was wrong. Weeping I turned to her, "I'm sorry Ann, I'm just very sad, depressed, and alone." I didn't mention what I planned to do once she packed up.

"I have known you for ten years," she said, "and have never seen you this depressed. Let's go in the den and talk for a while." The den was an addition full of windows looking out over my garden. The garden centerpiece was a twenty-foot waterfall cascading into a pond that held ornamental Japanese koi. It was a lovely setting to chat.

She began to ask questions about my sadness, and my answers spilled into hours. She patiently listened and shared the less-than-desirable aspects of her own life that she had to overcome to find peace within herself. I soaked at least one box of Kleenex. When I had said my piece, she looked at me and said, "If you want to change the way you see your life and release yourself from this pain, I suggest you call a therapist. There's one I know who I believe can help you." She wrote down a number and handed it to me. Our hands accidentally touched and stayed there for a moment. Looking me straight in the eye, Ann said, "Paul, I love you. Even if you think no one does, I do."

Her words were a wrecking ball.

She was right. I thought no one loved me.

Ann still had work to do, and she went back to the bathroom. I wonder what she was thinking back there. I slumped on the couch fixated on the phone number she had given me.

Thank You?

Frankly, I was a little perturbed that she had interrupted my plan. It was late in coming together, but it was coming together. I had a destiny with my father's heirloom, a date I didn't want to miss. Now this woman told me she loved me. My emotions were raw, and I was confused. I was conflicted about letting her down because of the risk she took to get in the messiness of my life. I sat with the phone number in hand staring at the pond.

Ann finished her work and packed up her supplies. I walked her to the door. As she left she looked earnestly at me, "*Promise* me you will call the number I gave you. I am certain he can help. Promise me you will call." I promised her as I assured myself I wouldn't. I closed the door gingerly. And when she was out of earshot, I locked the dead bolt.

I headed to the bedroom and got the heirloom out of the closet. I hadn't stopped to appreciate how black the barrel was. My suicide note rested in the next room, and I wasn't ready to make it a liar. But now I had two things in my way—a phone number on a scrap of paper and a human who had expressed love and concern. I felt like a kid who'd climbed the high dive fully intending to jump but couldn't. *What if she really does care about me that much? What if the therapist can help?*

I sat down on the couch again, my eyes floating between my backyard waterfall and the phone number. If I was going to call I needed to do it right away. I looked to my right and the cordless phone was there, clumsily dipped into the depression where two couch cushions met. I imagined it emanating some desperate cry for me to pick it up. All the while, the waterfall was a siren song calling me to the backyard. I decided to stop thinking about it, grasped at the phone, and plunked in the numbers.

"Um, yes, um. My name is Paul Wittwer. Ann gave me your phone number to make an appointment. I really need to talk to someone as soon as possible. Please call me back at . . ." I ended with a desperate recitation of my call-back number.

I hung up the phone calmly. If I made a mistake in calling and was disappointed, I told myself, I could always go back to the heirloom.

I had not told Ann of my plan to die that day, but I guess she sensed it. I've always wondered if she called the same number to give a heads-up because it wasn't long before I got a return call from a soothing baritone voice asking how he might be of assistance. It was just before Labor Day weekend, and he said he could only get to me the following Wednesday, September 5. I reluctantly made the appointment.

I struggled all day but put the Heirloom away in the closet once again. Somehow I was going to make it to that appointment if I could make it through the weekend. Ann called that night to check on me again. "I am better," I said. I still felt deathly awful. Technically, though, being alive is better than being dead, so I didn't feel like I was lying.

Understanding a Threat Decreases Its Power

The day of my appointment, September 5, 2001, I walked into a modest office. I sat down in a comfortable leather chair and

stared at the man with the baritone voice. He introduced himself as Dorney. He is a good six foot two, with dark brown hair,
a 1970s moustache, tender eyes, and a radiant smile that grips
your soul. His office contains tranquil art, lots of books, and
music memorabilia. Dorney, it turned, out was a therapeu-
tic songwriter who strums a great guitar. After a cordial introduction and finding conversational common ground, the
question-and-answer session began. I was such a lonely person
and had such poor self-esteem that I filled every breath with
something self-deprecating or painful from my past.

The hour flew, and there was something very different about
this therapist. He challenged my thoughts and presuppositions.
He didn't sleep through our session like one of my past therapists
had done on occasion. As our time came to a close, he asked if
I would like to make another appointment for the following
week. It felt good just to talk, better than I had felt in a long time.
It felt like the moment Ann said she loved me. So I made another
appointment. There was just something about Dorney that felt
like the promise of good results. That night Ann called to check
on me. "I am better," I said, and meant it a fraction more than
before. From then on, Ann and I didn't talk as much. I guess we
both figured her one degree purpose had been fulfilled in connecting me with Dorney. And I didn't have any wallpaper issues
to fix. We did stay distantly in touch during the journey ahead.

I love the line in the poem by T. S. Elliot, "I have measured
out my life in coffee spoons." I know it's a subjective interpre-
tation, but to me that line is about the small calculations we
make to add some semblance of order and control to our lives.

All the while, the fear we're trying to beat back with our coffee spoons, it lingers. That's how it was for me. The fears that haunted me and drove me to attempt suicide were no match for my coffee spoons. After that first appointment with Dorney, despite the sliver of hope, they whispered to me. The fear that had a stronghold in my life sensed an assailant in Dorney who could gain their territory, and they were launching a subtle counterattack to undo the hope.

To make it to my next appointment, I needed to stay busy. So I naturally went to work. I had let my consulting practice slip away—why keep it up when you're going to die? I made some calls and halfheartedly planted some seeds. In the mergers and acquisitions business, you can work for years on a deal that never comes through. Or you can be at the right place and the right time and make a million-dollar commission from a fifteen minute phone call. Neither of these would happen the week between my appointments. It was just the normal work between the poles, and it kept my mind occupied.

I made it to our second appointment at 10:00 a.m. on September 11, 2001 after I had just witnessed the second airplane hit the World Trade Center on television. Dorney had been in session all morning and did not even know of the attacks. He sent me home and canceled his remaining appointments. I've really struggled how to even mention this to you because I can't really do 9/11 justice. I can only point to the generalities, the distant pulsing and pain, not a string of specific, concrete moments. I wasn't there geographically—wasn't even close—but I can say that, like the rest of the world, the tension in Manhattan had seeped into my pores. When news stations ran clips of soaring bodies next to mirrored buildings, I trembled. Images pressed into my eyes like a seal on soft wax, detailed and symbolic. Three thousand souls died. I had all of my personal issues, and here was this collective issue we all dealt with. Like I said, I don't mean to claim myself as a victim of 9/11. Not in the way that there were literal victims. But my cocoon was so brittle, so susceptible. September 11, however distant, is a part of my story. It escalated what was already there.

I rescheduled with Dorney, and I made the third and fourth appointments too. It took a while to unload a life of difficulty on Dorney, starting with the cauldron and ending with the heirloom. I now realize why therapists get paid so well to listen— few would endure those hours for free. But still, it was my life in language, and if I was to find healing, the stage would need to be fully set.

During my fifth session, as I wrapped up the bleak narrative, Dorney interrupted my long-winded soliloquy and asked, "Paul has anyone ever discussed Post-Traumatic Stress Disorder with you?" I looked at him puzzled.

"You mean shell shock?" He shook his head in a confirming nod. "I have never been in the military," I said.

Dorney began to explain that the underlying cause of PTSD is trauma of any kind. And he had already heard me describe the challenges of death, illnesses, suicides, and calamities in my family. "I suspect," he said, "that you may have this mental illness." It was the first time I had ever heard those exact two words to explain me, *mental illness*.

Words are so unbelievably powerful. People say actions speak louder than words, but I disagree. If Ann hadn't said "I love you" who knows what action I would've taken. Words, at least in my experience, can speak inexplicable life. And when Dorney said "mental illness" it's like he handed me a decoder key, something to decipher myself.

Dorney continued to explain PTSD and its symptoms, things the credentialed pros call "comorbidities." These include obsessive-compulsive disorders and addictions. Everything he described about this stress syndrome and its comorbidities, I felt. I battered Dorney with questions. When a question got answered, I got a jolt of power, of empowerment. I was giddy with knowledge. And with the knowledge came slivered hope.

Dorney wiped his brow after what must've felt like a dissertation defense answering all my questions. He took a sip of water, looked me in the eye, and said, "If you are willing to do the work, I think I can introduce you to the life you have never known but have always deserved." He stopped in a pregnant pause to let the possibility dangle like a carrot. "But you will have to do the work."

"What does this 'work' involve?" I asked, holding up two tired air quotes.

He pointed to a device in the corner of his office. "That," he replied. "It's called EMDR, which stands for Eye Movement Desensitization and Reprocessing. With that machine, you will revisit every painful moment that has shaped you into this mess. Every hurt, every bit of wrongdoing, every shattering disappointment, every traumatic event. You will have to relive your life in this office and retrain your brain and emotions each step of the way."

There are moments in life where you think, *I'm paying for this?* This was one of those moments.

I would have to be reground in my life's crucible. The only other option was suicide. I pushed against the pain and pulled in the potential freedom and happiness. Dorney could see the conflict in my eyes, and he let me wrestle with it on my own terms.

After I left his office, I went straight home to find answers. I read page after page on websites of support groups and mental health organizations about Post-Traumatic Stress Disorder. Reading symptoms and accounts of other sufferers, I felt like I was reading a diary I had never taken the time to write. At one point I read the following sentence: "The likelihood of developing the disorder is greater when someone is exposed to multiple traumas or traumatic events early in life, especially if the trauma is long-term or repeated." Those words covered me like a blanket, suffocating and comforting.

In my research, I learned the likely origin of my recently discovered intelligence. It is an obsessive-compulsive disorder known as "hypervigilance," which I had likely been developing since I was a child. One friend of mine describes it like this: hypervigilance is a person waiting for a tiger to pounce but it never does. In fact, the tiger is nowhere even close. It's what makes people cross the street to avoid a suspicious passerby. To choose, for some gut-level reason, the aisle seat over the window, and next to that man instead of this woman. Hypervigilance also makes it difficult to sleep, a gun under your pillow in the one-in-a-gazillion chance a Tokyo street gang breaks into your Oklahoma home. People with this disorder will *never* drop their guard, not even for an instant. It's a steady drip of adrenaline, the weird sensation of tonguing a battery.

Hypervigilance also manifests in a sort of divination power, the ability to gauge people's mettle and make-up. A decent glance with some eye contact, and I could peer into a person's soul. A little conversation and I could tell someone his birth order, the color of his car, the size of his clothes, inseam of trousers, and weight within three pounds. I was an everyday carnival freak. And the better I got with it over the years, the spookier it became for others around me. In business meetings, I did not have to take notes, yet I could tell each person up to twelve exactly what they had said in the order they said it. Years later.

Alongside my own research, I was reading an academic-looking tome about PTSD that Dorney had given me in our last session. I was anxious to determine whether I should go through with the work he recommended, I picked it up and did not put it down until I read the whole thing. There seemed to be a road map there. Examples of Vietnam veterans and Oklahoma City bombing survivors who had suffered years of pain. After a few sessions of the same "work" that Dorney had recommended with his machine, they were beginning to enjoy life again. Could it be possible for me to have, as Dorney had stated, the life that I had never known but always deserved?

When I considered this path, I was forty-nine years old, pushing 250 pounds, and diabetic with high triglycerides. I was a walking lipid. I also suffered from fibromyalgia so bad that if I talked on the phone for more than ten minutes, I could not straighten out my arm without manually pulling the muscles in my bicep and forearm with my other hand. I admitted to myself that there was no place to go but up, that I couldn't continue to live as I had if there was an alternative. I picked up the phone and called Dorney.

"Dorney, this is Paul. I'm ready to do the work."

"If you are truly willing to do the work, you will have more peace of mind and financial success than you have ever imagined," he replied.

The Only Way Out Is Through

There I am sitting in a chair in Dorney's office, my forearms resting by my side holding a small bar in each hand. Dorney sets up a tripod in front of me at eye level and places on top of it a long, rectangular box filled with equally spaced LED lights. He turns it on momentarily to make sure it's working properly, and the lights oscillate from end to end, with a trail of fading light following like a comet tail. Dorney asks me to focus on following the lights moving back and forth and to relax. Then we begin. Dorney asks me questions, the simple things to get us in the groove, like the beginning of a lie detector test.

"What is your name?"

"Paul Wittwer." The lights are going back and forth slowly.

"What day is it?"

"September 26."

As he asks questions to focus my thoughts on the challenges in my life, I'm watching the light bar and the comet tail. When the comet reaches one end, the thing I'm holding in my left hand gives me a slight pulse. When it reaches the other end, I feel another light pulse in my right hand. Back and forth it goes, pulsing and pulsing, while Dorney asks and asks.

The lights and questions are designed to get me into my deepest memories and feelings, the places where the weeds of my trouble popped up and flayed roots into the soil of my brain. When my eyes stop following the lights, Dorney knows that I'm ready. He seizes the moment.

"Paul, what are you seeing?" I'm staring blankly, almost hypnotically.

It all felt so strange. In a flash of seconds, I would see images of my life moving fluidly through different ages as if I were literally present. From age seven, to thirty-one, back to thirteen then forty-one. I could feel all of the experiences, and intensely. Dorney kept asking, "What are you seeing?" and he would coach me through each moment, teaching me to retrain my visceral, uncontrollable emotional responses to each trauma, each hurt. I responded as best I could, but often the images caused me horrendous emotional pain. I would yell out an answer. "I see my father lying on the floor in front of me with his first heart attack." And from there I would begin to wail.

———

I was retraining my brain to feel different things about my past, and those new feelings would bring me freedom in the present and future. It was nearly unbearable, yes. But it was progress, and that was a new, exhilarating feeling.

I mean, I was so enlivened by the feeling of progress that I ran headlong into my own storm, a tornado chaser unafraid of the eye. We stepped up the pace to one, two, and then three sessions a week. I began to see my life in split seconds, a time-lapse photography presentation of my existence. I started a spreadsheet to chart the traumatic events of my life in a continuous timeline. Then I had a stunning revelation. I don't mean to get clinical on you, but it became increasingly clear that every important decision I had made in business, life, and love had been based on a "false coping self," the person I let the world see to protect the real person cowering on the inside.

Through our sessions, I kept discovering and revisiting events and retraining my brain. It was grueling, tiring stuff. But I was committed. I also realized that, in some sense, I had my illnesses to thank: the obsessive compulsiveness that had contributed to my lunge toward suicide was the very thing that kept me from getting out the Heirloom. The OCD couldn't handle the wallpaper, and the wallpaper led to my salvation through Ann's risky expression of love. If there was a life that I had always deserved but had never known, then I was going to find it! To get there, though, I would have to go through the life I had already.

Water Aerobics

At the onset of our sessions, Dorney had told me that if I wanted to have a good life emotionally, I had to take care of myself and have a healthy body too. Healthiness is a package deal, and my overweight, diabetic body needed as much attention as my mind and emotions. Plus, I had made a blind commitment to my endocrinologist to do whatever he asked of me for a healthy life. I had to eat right, of course, but I also needed to exercise. I chose water aerobics.

Water aerobics is often considered exercise for the lumpy. Old men and women squeeze themselves into synthetic suits and practice synchronized routines, their weightless limbs trailing back and forth in the buoyant water. The first day I joined a class, I was clearly one of the youngest members. Thus, I was the stud. It was kind of fun. But there's something pensive about moving methodically in water. It gets you in a meditative state.

One day during a class, I simply stopped moving and looked, I'm sure, entranced to my senior partners. I was caught up thinking about my therapy sessions, my progress, and what it all meant. One lady who knew what I was trying to accomplish saw me and swam over.

"What's wrong, Paul?"

I snapped to and realized I was in a swimming pool.

"Oh, um," I stammered as I began choking up, "I've lost my whole life to an illness over which I have no control." I have a gift for blurting personal information like it's a casual hello.

She looked at me earnestly and tenderly, grandmotherly even. Then she straightened herself up like she was projecting a strength onto me.

"How old are you, Paul?" she asked sternly.

"I'm almost fifty."

She paused with a face full of consolation and wisdom, looked me dead in the eye, and said, "Be thankful that you found out now and not at seventy." The rebuke in her voice lasted mere moments. She winked and floated away, buoyant.

One Degree

When you don't experience much hope in life, you *know* when you feel it, you clutch it close and tattoo it on your skin. Here's the hope that bowled me over: Ann, my wallpaper friend, and Dorney—they are brother and sister. I didn't learn this until three months into my therapy. Dorney lived in my neighborhood, less than two-tenths of a mile from my house, just down the street. But to find out that Ann had referred me to her own brother to help me find a new life, it was too much kismet, the kind of overblown coincidence that registers more like divine intervention than luck.

I had known Ann for nearly ten years, and she had worked in my house several times during those years. I had been carrying my illness all of my life and never once did I know of her brother or that he was a family therapist. Was it possible that for ten years I had been one degree from finding the life I dreamed about? What is more, Ann had come to my home at a time when I was ready to give up. She was there that day, talked to me, loved me. Ever since my riddled arrival in this world with the curse of our family thickening our air like fog, this was the first time I that something good was pushing forward, was fighting on my behalf. It was an emboldening thought.

Walmart in a Gurney

While I was hustling through my therapy sessions and going miles and miles in place on a treadmill to lose weight, a little inconvenience came my way. Plantar warts. Yes, warts. I'm not crazy about the word either, believe me. I still remember Billy holding toads over my face with threats of a lifetime of bumpy disfigurement. But I was going to have to deal with the warts on my feet mainly because I was diabetic. And to a person with diabetes, feet are everything. They're the first thing to go, and when they do you know you're in trouble. In my mind, I would be completely immobilized if my diabetes headed south and I had warts. I made an appointment with a podiatrist and scheduled surgery for both my feet Friday, December 21.

I had to do both feet at the same time because I was flat broke. Electing to do both feet at once was all about the deductible, which reset January 1, and I had no money to pay a new deductible in the new year. I won't go into details about the surgery. It happened and that was that. A taxi took me home, and since I had no one there to care for me, I had to do it all on my own. Bandages, soaking, rewrapping, medications, all of it. I think this would be tough enough if I were perfectly fit. But I was overweight, truly. My feet and I were not friends too well acquainted. In fact, we didn't see each other much.

Three months into my therapy, in the midst of my foot surgery planning, Dorney suggested that I throw an open house a couple of weeks before Christmas and actually have people over to enjoy their company. He said it could be a small crowd, just a few folks. I did just as he suggested and it provided a major breakthrough for me in my therapy. I had become so reclusive and full of social anxiety in my beautiful little home that I had shut everyone and everything out. The place was like a well-appointed crypt. However, on the day of my open house and the days following I was beginning to feel a sense of relief that I could come out of my burrow and could enjoy a life I had never known. Seeing myself differently and living!

I had become so thankful for the few other people in my life that one morning I dragged myself bandaged and oozing to Walmart to buy Christmas gifts with a fifteen dollar budget. I should have been on gurney.

Groggy, sore, and bulging, I got out of bed on Sunday December 23. I wrapped my feet, put on my surgical boots, and tiptoed out of my house. I put my tender foot to the gas pedal and headed to Walmart to do some Christmas shopping. About that flat broke thing, I literally had no cash. None. No change jars for the little runs to the convenience store. No secret moola for the impulse buy. My couch had already made its full donation to the cause.

For my friends, I bought cookies, a movie, and a can of corn on my credit card. That last gift seems strange, I know. But it was an inside joke for me and the recipient. I don't categorically recommend giving people corn for Christmas.

My trip to Walmart, what it represented, was most fun. It felt good to think about other people, do something spontaneously that gave back the love and attention they had shown me. But it was a quick reprieve.

If you're buying a can of corn on your credit card, you might have some more significant life needs to attend to. And I certainly did. On January 9, 2002 I went to my satellite branch, the Waffle House, and considered all of my options. As I sat in the corner booth with a sweet, down-home waitress offering coffee, I looked at my flagging income and my Kentucky home I could no longer afford. Truth be told, I was on the brink of financial ruin, and I had to do some checkbook triage to stay afloat. With my intense process with Dorney in full swing and the myriad physical needs I was trying to attend to, there wasn't much left over at the end of the month to take care of life's basics. I had to make a choice. Would I invest in my health or in the trappings of a "normal" life?

The Great Repossession

I had promised my Dad when I was young that I would always protect my credit. Through all of my bad choices and circumstances, I had never been late on a payment, defaulted, or declared bankrupt. I was not going to start now. I resolved to sell my Kentucky house and auction off all of my belongings to pay down debt, protect my credit, and keep moving toward my new life without pain.

The motorhome I purchased less than a year before was now going to become my home of last resort. I called a realtor and an auction company, and as I inched into the liquidation process, relief and excitement began to bubble and erupt inside me. Getting rid of my stuff felt like a final handshake good-bye to some of the monuments of my illness. I knew I could get by there. I was on a new quest to prepare for homelessness and a Walmart-hopping life.

Dates were locked in with the realty company and auctioneer. The day of the auction was odd. Four hundred people descended on my broken palace and scoured the rooms one by one. I watched like a farmer who couldn't stop the locusts. A few days later the auction company had an itemized list of sale prices and a check for me to retrieve. I headed straight to the bank with that paper and handed the funds directly to the teller to pay down and stay current on my debts. I never read the itemized list—I didn't want to know what my life was worth wholesale. All that remained were the fish in my pond and two bronze statues that did not sell, one a five-foot saxophone player and the other a six-foot alligator. My pond guy agreed to take the statues on consignment.

I needed cash to live on, so I advertised the koi in the Louisville newspaper as a collection, and a couple visiting from Baltimore happened upon the ad. They came to the house and made me an offer with one condition. I had to deliver the fish alive in Baltimore 620 miles away. I called my fish guy, and we developed a plan. The Baltimore buyers agreed to receive the fish in one month, on May 1. I can't express how important and fraught with risk this transportation would be. I had absolutely *no money*. My ability to stay afloat was contingent on belly-down fish.

In the month leading up to my eastbound journey, I focused on finding gainful employment and wrapping up my sessions with Dorney. That I was broke as broke could be, it hit me hard like aftershave on a nicked face. I had to find work again if I ever wanted to crawl out of homelessness. And I had to do it healthily lest I slip back to some dark tendencies and memories, the ones that Dorney had equipped me to overcome.

When my mergers and acquisitions pipeline was active, I had a contact in Daytona Beach, Florida, Lamar Williams. He was my ace in the hole in those days. He owned and operated the American Motorcycle Institute, AMI, Inc. and was my connection to a system of technical schooling for cars, trucks, and diesels. And ever since my boyhood days, standing on tiptoes to peek at the inscrutable guts of an engine, I had always been drawn to the business of teaching vehicles. While Dad worked on the truck, I was always underfoot zipping on the wheeled floor creeper you use to roll up under the chassis.

With Lamar's input and my own research of the post-secondary for-profit technical school industry, I learned of a group in the northeast that could be a good lead for acquisition opportunities. So, on April 5, I called Lincoln Educational Services, Lamar's recommendation, and asked to speak with David Carney, Chairman and CEO. When we spoke, he shared some of their vision for acquisitions and growing their business, and I asked if he would be interested in meeting in person. He was, and I told him that I would be in his parking lot at three o'clock in the afternoon that Thursday. I could hear his brow furrow over the phone, and he asked why I would meet in his parking lot. I told him to watch his email for the answer.

I sent him a picture of my motorhome with a Jeep hitched behind. He called me up immediately, "What's this?"

"This is where I live. I will see you on Thursday." I chuckle to think what this guy might have been thinking at that moment. When you think "mergers and acquistions," images of Manhattan men at least six foot three inches with beautiful hair striding in pinstripe suits probably come to mind. Maybe that's what David imagined too. I'm a bit more pedestrian than that. My office was a Waffle House.

The day I arrived, I sent an email to Dave from the parking lot. The subject line read, "The Eagle Has Landed" and the body was a sole line with no closing signature, "Look out your window."

———

On the morning of May 1, I unplugged from a KOA at six o'clock and headed in my mobile home to my liquidated house. My pond guy met me there, and we began capturing the fish, storing them in heavy duty bags that we placed in special freezer cardboard boxes. The bags were filled with pure oxygen and covered with dry ice. This put the fish into a sleep state and would keep them alive, assuming I could get to Baltimore that same day. Without live fish I could not make the May payments for the motorhome and Jeep.

All of the fish were loaded, and I was ready to release the mooring line that had kept me latched to my old life. I fired up the coach and took one last long look at the house. I didn't know what would be ahead of me. I knew one thing for certain. I would have to financially survive, though I wasn't quite sure how that would happen.

Despite the uncertainty, I looked back on where I was months before with my only friend, the heirloom. I had certainly progressed. And though it wasn't quite the dream life, it was exciting and fresh and hopeful. I was beginning to see the fruits of Dorney's promise about a new life. It stretched out before me like a long highway, and I was just getting started. The next stop on my journey would be on the eastern seaboard, to Baltimore. And the drive there would be one long prayer for my fish.

3

An Old World
Made New

I drove past neighbors' homes as most of them still slept. I was taken aback by the beautiful normality of what I was seeing, of this human community I was entering under new circumstances. I was assured that somehow I belonged with them, that I could do something and be something complementary to them. As I left the city limits, I gazed out the motorhome window and imagined my house, picked clean like an elephant's rib cage in the Serengeti, fading in the background. The blinds were shut and no lights were on. There was no sign of movement. It was the dawn of a new day in my new life with sunshine ahead and darkness behind.

When you become free of stuff, life becomes alarmingly basic. You wonder how you'll get by without your fancy coffee machine, or you lament the loss of your routine, sitting down to watch the evening news. It's like fasting for a day or two: you're alive but you're miserable, irritable, and constantly thinking about things you don't have. During the ride, my focus was Baltimore, delivering the fish, collecting a check, and surviving until the next day. In the previous weeks there had been so much momentum, so many doings, that the road trip started to feel excruciatingly slow. The euphoria of leaving something and going into the unknown gave way to reality, and the reality was I had no solid idea of how I was going to survive beyond the money from the fish.

During the weeks leading up to my departure, I had decided to develop some routines that would give my homelessness some normalcy. Since the 9/11 attacks, I got up every morning and watched the *Today Show* with Katie, Ann, Matt and Al. They gave me comfort, so I planned every morning in the motorhome to see the beginning of each show. The cast of the *Today Show* became my imaginary family, a way to hedge against the loneliness that would find me eventually in my Walmart-hopping life on the road.

My Secret Recipe

The road is a great place to think. As I drove, I kept mulling over a hero of mine, a man who was particularly famous when you live in Kentucky. As a child growing up in rural Kentucky in the '50s and '60s, there were three living legends everyone knew about, Adolph Rupp, the legendary coach of the University of Kentucky basketball team, Muhammad Ali, and my favorite, Colonel Harland Sanders, a near-native Kentuckian. The Colonel is an unlikely hero, but his story combines perseverance, vision, tenacity, smarts, and selflessness that model the way I hope to live.

Born in 1890 to a poor farm family in Henryville, Indiana, seventeen miles north of Louisville, Harland became head of the household at the age of six after his father died. At twelve, his new stepfather did not take kindly to him and his siblings. Harland was abused, and as a result he left home and school in the seventh grade. For the record, Harland blamed his jettison on mathematics.

His career path was something I could relate to. It was more like a cow path in small Kentucky towns, a meandering thing that eventually got to market. Harland could hold a job only a few months or a year at most. His many jobs included collecting fares on streetcars, caring for mules on cargo boats, tending deck on a riverboat, assisting a blacksmith, and working in the rail yard driving spikes, laying rail, and stoking coal-fired steam engines. After some brief runs with life insurance and tire sales, Harland decided to acquire his own filling station.

Like a lot of other things in those days, though, the Great Depression did it in. He rebounded with a move to Corbin, Kentucky and took over a Shell station. The station was a success and Sanders saw the need to add a motel to the property that he called Sander's Court. It was there that he began serving meals in a small room attached to the service station. His fried chicken became local legend almost instantly. It didn't take Harland long to realize you can board a person one night but you can feed them three times a day. Locals and visitors from nearby towns came in droves. He expanded the dining area and renamed the establishment Sander's Café and Shell Station.

Harland was a man who understood a need when he saw one. He had great business instincts, tenacity, and perseverance. Most important of all, he was unafraid to fail. At the Sander's

Café, he perfected the method and flavors of the chicken. This is when the "secret recipe" was born, and so were the cooking methods he developed to cut cook time down from thirty minutes to eight.

Business boomed, offers to buy the restaurant were made and declined. And then President Eisenhower created the vision for the national interstate highway system and soon work began on I-75 that would reroute the highway that gave Corbin its lifeblood. The change forced Sanders to liquidate the restaurant to cover the debts, but he believed the chicken was his meal ticket at age sixty-four. With only his first Social Security check for $105, he loaded his station wagon with his pressure cooker and the eleven secret ingredients and set out to sell the rights to use or franchise his famous recipe. Sanders would stop at respected and successful local restaurants, prepare the chicken free using the special recipe, and then let the owner decide if he wished to acquire a franchise at a fee of five cents a chicken plus purchase of his special recipe ingredients. The rest is history as it is known to most of the world.

The Colonel was far more personal in my life, more than an image on a paper bucket or plastic sign. As an elementary and high school student, I awoke each morning to read the paper with my father before I went to school. The business section was always the first read, and I followed the development of Kentucky Fried Chicken, the Colonel's ultimate sale of the company, and his life as its spokesperson. When his autobiography, *Life as I Have Known It Has Been Finger Lickin' Good* came out in 1974, I studied the backstory of his challenged life too.

When the Colonel died in December 1980 at age ninety, I was twenty-eight years old and living in Evansville, Indiana. I read of his death in the paper, and it said his body would be lying in state in an open casket for public viewing at the Kentucky Fried Chicken headquarters in Louisville. Off I went to pay my respects in person.

I walked in the lobby slowly and respectfully. The foyer had a quiet, somber air. As I crossed the threshold, I could see his casket in the distance just outside his office. Strangely, I was the only person there, like this first face-to-face meeting was specially arranged. Approaching the casket, I could spy his familiar white suit and black string tie. There I was, just me and the Colonel for more than fifteen minutes, alone together. I stood before him in reverence, gazing at his face, thinking of all he had endured as a child and all that he had accomplished late in his life from his midsixties to his death at ninety. In those moments I *knew* that someday I would need the personal strength and fortitude of the Colonel to pull my life from the bowels of failure.

I tried to photograph the Colonel's image with my mind, to firmly plant the power of his perseverance in my memory. Nearly twenty-two years later, as I approached fifty, that day had come and I had to conjure the Colonel.

At the wheel of the motorhome, burning a path to Baltimore, I was running the Colonel's story through my mind drawing inspiration from it. As he hovered on my dash right above the console, I thought about his secret recipe of eleven herbs and spices and how he had used a pressure cooker to speed his delicacy to the customer. I needed to develop my recipe for I was certainly in the pressure cooker. By the time I reached Baltimore, I had my recipe clearly *in* my head and committed it to paper.

1. We are all one degree from giving and receiving hope and help.
2. Treat everyone with kindness and respect.
3. Charge into the unknown and accept every challenge as an opportunity.
4. Always be generous.
5. Strive to make every relationship more positive and long-lasting.
6. Turn disadvantages into advantages.
7. Work with and for people who embrace similar life and business goals.
8. Always give yourself grace.

The Colonel did it, I can do it too!

Fed by the Fishes

I swung in the drive of the Baltimore fish owners. It was dusk, so we didn't waste too many pleasantries. We headed straight back to the pond, and with the owners hovering over me, I released the koi into their new home. And I waited.

When a creature that can breathe under water starts coming to the surface gasping for air, something is probably wrong. That's exactly what happened. Apparently, the owner had added an antibacterial treatment to the water, and it was killing the fish.

I got the owner's emergency air pump and hurriedly aerated the pond. I sat for over an hour into the night watching dollar signs floating around in the dark water. After a while, when our triage seemed to be working, I was given a check. The buyer informed me the fish would have to survive the night for the check to be good. I drove to a nearby Walmart and to a sleepless night. I prayed for the fish and for a gracious extension of some means to live. I returned the next morning. The fish had survived. I immediately drove to the bank and cashed the check.

It was May 2, 2002. I had no pets, no house, no furniture, utilities, neighbors, or companions. I had more than five thousand dollars in cash from the koi, which would soon become payments for the motorhome, Jeep, and credit card. With the remainder, I estimated I had four weeks of living expenses. I had four weeks to figure out what would happen next or face bankruptcy and total liquidation.

Putting My Recipe to the Test

It is said that necessity is the mother of all invention. And I had a desperate need to reinvent my life and generate some new income. I sat in my motorhome, my elbows resting on the oversized steering wheel, and decided to revisit the acquisitions lead

I had cultivated just weeks earlier. Dave, my contact at Lincoln, was the kind of person I wanted to work with under my new secret recipe. With the fish at the their new home— and me, with no home to go back to—I was finally at a place where I could give my energies full tilt to generating income.

I hauled in the early morning from Baltimore and headed north. I was passing into business hours as I rolled through southern Pennsylvania when I called Dave. He took my call, and we met that day. We picked up right where we left and resumed discussing their growth plans and how I may be able to help. The good news was that they were interested in working with me. The bad news, however, was that they were only interested in doing so with a success fee basis. Meaning, I would get paid when a deal finally happened, the papers were signed, and the keys were handed over. I tried to keep my composure while my heart sank like a feather in a rainstorm. My one-month timeline was not conducive to the lead times of the mergers and acquisitions business. I did not dare tell them I was broke—I simply asked for their acquisition criteria. After we identified a few targets, I practically sprinted to my coach, peeled rubber out of the parking lot, and drove straight to Exton, Pennsylvania, making cold calls to the first school on the way.

I arrived that evening and spent the night in a Super Target parking lot. The following day, a Friday, with the school owners off campus, I decided to sign up for a tour as a prospective student's parent. I'm sure the young man who did the tour was perplexed when I kept asking him unusual questions about the school, not the sort of things a student would care to know. But still, I was researching, and I wasn't going to let a day pass.

The following day would begin my first weekend living full-time in the coach. It was unsettling and exciting. To keep pushing forward, I had to look at each day as an unfolding adventure taking me places I had never seen. There was an electrification to it, which seems to be the way things always begin. You embark on some impossible task, you ask the girl to marry you, you start a new job. But where will you be ten, twenty years from the embarkation? The beginning is always the fun part—it's the middle that lags.

The next prospect was in York, due west from Exton. I looked over the maps and highlighted attractions and amusements for the trip. It just so happened that my route traveled directly through Lancaster County—Amish country. I once saw a program about the Amish. The narrator recounted their heritage and their history while images of barn raisings, horse-drawn buggies, and general industriousness floated in and out of the screen. Apart from the antiquated clothes and the unconventional facial hair, I really had a deep affinity for the Lancaster communities I visited. Have you ever built something from start to finish? Watched seeds turn to sprouts, then plants, then food? Known how magnificent a car's horsepower can be when you've closely felt the immensity of just one during a gallop? There is still a romantic charm to their lives, a living tableau from 1836.

Being in Lancaster calmed my nerves despite grazing horse-drawn buggies on the highway roadsides as I drove. It put me in a quieted frame of mind for my upcoming meeting. That Monday, it turned out that Thursday was the earliest time we could meet. So I dropped anchor in a Walmart parking lot for three days and continued my exploration of Pennsylvania.

Over the next three days, I drank in the history at the battlefield at Gettysburg, a soil rich in stories and a wind carrying the voices of the admirably departed. I ambled in awe at the Harley-Davidson manufacturing plant. Between the Amish, Civil War, and Harley-Davidson, I felt like I was seeing a real America. In a matter of hours and days I moved from our religious ancestry to our nationalistic history straight on through the industrial revolution. *This*, I thought at one whimsical moment, *is worth living for.* My suicide attempt hadn't come to mind often since I'd left home. And when it did, it was often cast in the light of thankfulness rather than regret.

But still, there were downsides. Every day I woke up fearful and disoriented. It still hadn't registered that I was temporarily living in Pennsylvania, and apparitions of cannon shot, horse-drawn carriages, and Hogs were dancing around in my brain. I felt like an intoxicated time traveler.

Nor did it help that every morning, around three o'clock, the Walmart parking lot was cleaned by street sweepers. To deal with my genuine anxiety, I covered my bed with one of the patchwork quilts my grandmother had made. I also started thinking of the coach as a tree house, my private hideaway place from everything. I even gave the coach a silly name, Kamp Kandu, making it more joyful to refer to it as my home. I know this seems a little elementary, like I'm drinking a warm glass of milk and dunking a cookie every night before bedtime. But I'll say this: it worked, and I needed all the help I could get.

I had my initial meeting on Thursday, and the initial talks were underway. The next three weeks were a back-and-forth between York and Exton with prep between the two schools. I got to know the bends in the road, the mile marker signs. I befriended the equally spaced white lines and the highway patrol speed traps. I knew to the last drop the miles-per-gallon of the motorhome. There was a wonderful routine to it all, something that helped me feel grounded and measured despite my crazy deadline before bankruptcy.

I could hear loneliness and sadness whispering from trees lining the highways, from the farm houses hidden in the fields where families gathered around home-cooked meals. I knew I had to find a way to develop a sense of community wherever I went, or the isolation and loneliness were going to eat me alive.

Greet the Greeter

If you have ever visited a Walmart, you are probably familiar with the person who stands near the door wearing the trademark blue vest with all the flair. You know who I am talking about, the Walmart Greeter, the person you quickly acknowledge while they say hello and push a cart out in front of you. Because I was living in Walmart parking lots, it was only natural that I would consider these folks my family wherever I parked. So, whenever I would claim my territory a long way off in the lot, I would march right up to the stores and greet *them*.

But here's the thing about Walmart greeters, they're kind of a diverse, predictable group. Often they're retired or engaging in different ways. And I related to them all, felt an affinity with the swath of people who, it seemed, had been pulled from the fringes. I would walk up to my soon-to-be family with an extended hand, spy their name tag, and say, "Hi, Walter. My name is Paul. I *live* in the parking lot."

It was a funny cultural experiment because these greeters don't often get past hello with the hoards of shoppers. They would usually ask in reply, "Are you passing through?" A very natural question that gave me the benefit of the doubt. And with a peaceful half smile, I would reply, "No. I live in the parking lot." You would be surprised how open people become when you're willing to drop pretenses and how rewarding it is when you glide beyond the facade we all keep. When you take a moment to ask a question of a stranger that shows genuine interest, it's like they're drawn out of a cave of isolation and loneliness, tempted by the prospect of meaningful interaction with others. We're all that way, really. And those who seem unresponsive to the goodness and love of their fellow man are only pretending. I should know—I did it for years. The Walmart greeters were my family, my friends. And with a few simple questions, I got to hear the never-before-told life stories of dozens of strangers. Their lives, their tenacity, were sustenance to my life-weary self. The stories of triumph and tragedy I gleaned from the greeters were astonishment and encouragement gift-wrapped for me.

Finally, the Thursday came when the leaders from Lincoln would meet the team from the Exton school on their own turf. I was buzzing with excitement. After the school tour, the Lincoln entourage asked if I wanted to join them for lunch. Discussing business over a meal was a two-bird-one-stone proposition for me—I was nearly out of cash, and I was dying to know what they thought.

It was a beautiful spring day as we sat outside a quaint restaurant. The guys expressed their appreciation for my opening doors at two schools. But they regrettably explained that neither would be good fits for their organization at that time. I dropped my spoon into my French onion soup. I had tried my best during my three weeks in Pennsylvania, and there I was broke, with no prospects, and a half-eaten bowl of soup. Oh, and it was my birthday.

I could not contain my emotions any longer. Taking a deep breath, I told them gently, "Today is a good day and a bad day."

"What is the good part," they asked.

"Today is my birthday, and I am fifty years old."

"Happy birthday," they replied. I was not thinking about cake and candles.

"The bad part is that I am totally broke, and everything I own is in the parking lot in my motorhome and Jeep." I could see it on their faces, the shock and surprise. Though I had never given them any reason to think I was wealthy, I believe they thought my old motorhome was an eccentric choice in what should've been a high-powered life.

They were both very gracious in their response. They didn't prod or pry or leave—all of which I was thankful for. And after a few odd moments with the sound of coffee spoons clinking ceramic cups, Dave looked at me and said, "If you can get to Nashville, there is a school there, Nashville Auto Diesel College. We have been trying to get on the phone with them for two years, and they will not return our calls. If you can get a deal going with them, there will be a small fortune in it for you." I looked him in the eyes and could see his sincerity. I could tell that this was not a nicety or consolation prize meant for pity. No, for whatever reason, they were truly interested in me. After another few moments, they asked for the check. I had no time to lose. "Well, I am off to Nashville," I said with a brisk walk to my motorhome.

But before I could start my southbound trip, I had to get some work done on the motorhome. I spent the evening of my fiftieth birthday among a bunch of broken-down trucks at a Cummins diesel shop in Harrisburg, where my celebration dinner was McDonald's, a Big Mac and fries. I reminisced about Dorney and Ann. Momentarily, my mind drifted to my parents as I walked through the timeline of recent days. How was it that my life had come to this?

As dusk went to night and the parking area grew silent, my heart pounded with determination. I crumpled the sandwich wrapper and walked my tray to the trash bin. People were coming and going in day-old clothes and work boots buying drinks and candy bars. Their feet shuffled and thudded against the concrete floors and through the disheveled aisles. I pushed out the swinging door in the late dusk and walked between rows of eighteen wheelers parked for the night. The lines of yellow daylights were shining in the oil-slicked pools of standing water. I climbed into the motorhome with a slight bellyache and full-blown heartache. But there was something deeper too, some vestigial light burning. It was a resolve like the Colonel's, and I latched onto it desperately. I swung it madly at my sadness as I brushed my teeth and slipped into bed. I fell asleep as that battle waged, staring at the ceiling with a racing mind until the exhaustion of the last three weeks finally overtook me.

Dave

I drove out of Pennsylvania watching the horizon move out as I advanced toward it. There was a Rice Krispie Bar warming on my dash, and the soundtrack from *O Brother, Where Art Thou?* was blaring, "Oh I, I am a man, of constant sorrows. I've seen trouble all my days."

As early as I was able, I cold-called the president of Nashville Auto Diesel College. He was not in, and I had to leave a voicemail. I take pride in my tenacity and ability to get people to call me back. Often when I cold-call and leave a message, I inform the prospect that they may as well call me back because I am known as "The Pleasant Pest." The following day, he called me back. We discussed Lincoln's interest in acquiring his school, and arranged for me come to Nashville to visit the school June 4, the week following my first days in the motorhome.

"Where will you stay?" he asked.

"Where's your closest Walmart?" I replied. He seemed a little stunned.

"Really?" he said after a brief pause, as if to call my bluff.

"Yes," I replied without wavering.

Politely he gave me some general directions to my Nashville home, a Walmart on Gallatin Road north of the school.

My small cash reserves were dwindling. In the days before Memorial Day, I developed a plan with my banker whereby, if I did not have any success in Nashville, he would *consider* working with me on an orderly liquidation of my motorhome and Jeep outside of bankruptcy. They would *consider* allowing me to carry unsecured debts because I had never been late, delinquent, or bankrupt. Additionally they would consider loaning me up to six thousand dollars for purchase of a station wagon so I could have something in which to live, work, and sleep. Knowing that I was on a very high wire with an awfully unsecure net, I began looking into homeless and men's shelters in the Louisville area. If I were to be homeless, I at least wanted it to be on my home turf, not in a new city. It was sobering to think that only sixty days ago I had owned a beautiful home and now I was looking at shelters.

I finally met with the NADC president and his mother who were partial owners. We had a positive meeting, and I had a foundational knowledge about the school. They were very interested in a possible deal, but they were reluctant too. The history of the school was also the history of their family. And though they knew they wouldn't keep that legacy forever, it was still difficult to consider letting it go. It was my job to help them willingly open their hands. Over the next two days, they reached the conclusion that they wanted to sell the school to Lincoln if the right deal could be made. I was in an absolute frenzy getting the right people to the table so we could have the conversation.

At this point, my four weeks were up. Though I was making progress, I was running out of cash and the credit available to me on my card. I was living on $1.88 a pound artificial crabmeat and hardly running my generator. I wanted to conserve fuel to get the motorhome back to Louisville if all failed in Nashville. I lived nervously at Walmart waiting for the meeting between Lincoln and NADC.

When the day finally came, I and three executives piled into my Jeep Liberty to go to the Nashville school. The Lincoln execs were sitting on their luggage. We met the NADC owners for dinner and the next day had a tour of the school.

The following day seemed the longest of my life as we walked the school grounds. They showed us the vaulting buildings full of dismantled diesel engines, the dormitories. We waded through a sea of mostly young men in "uniform," grayish suits that marked them future mechanics. We met the staff in the central office building, an old colonial house that was once a solitary residence in the now-urban neighborhood.

I could tell NADC had the right vibe for the Lincoln execs. When we loaded back into the Jeep I sensed their excitement as we drive to the airport. When we stopped at the skycap curb, Dave handed me a miracle. It was just an envelope, but it soon became a miracle.

"What is this?" The envelope rested lazily in my hand as I searched Dave's face for any sign about what was happening.

"Just open it." I could see a brightness on his face, an

anticipation. I knew this couldn't be all bad, so I went ahead and opened the envelope. I tentatively lifted the flap. I could've been a mother during war receiving a telegram from the government, I was so transfixed. Inside, barely revealed by the v-shaped center of the envelope, was a small slip of paper. I pinched a check between my thumb and forefinger and pulled it out.

Inside the envelope was a check for five thousand dollars. I stared at Dave unable to speak. He said the Lincoln team wanted to help me keep going and to stay on the job in Nashville. This check would be the first of many as a stipend to keep the deal alive. Dave asked me to give him a per diem amount for each night I had spent in the motorhome, meals, fuel, and mileage, and I would be reimbursed each month. On top of that, he wanted to calculate a consulting fee for my services and payment terms *when* (not if) we closed the deal in Nashville.

I wept openly.

I grabbed Dave in an awkward, blubbery hug without reserve. I didn't care how it looked. I finally let him out of my bear grip, mumbled a "good night" and a "talk to you soon" and returned, shocked, to the Walmart. I walked up the extending stairs of the coach elated and stunned. God had delivered a one degree miracle through Dave.

Share the Love

I had spent so many days on the precipice of homelessness and bankruptcy that it felt odd to be a little farther back from the ledge. What would it mean to not hesitate at the gas pump? To make a car payment without worrying about my crabmeat supply? To not live on artificial crabmeat?

It had been a little over a month since I had delivered the fish to Baltimore. The only human touch I had experienced were handshakes in the windswept entrances of Walmarts and a brief hug with Dave. I had learned that I could survive, that I was friendly enough to make friends, that I had the courage and tenacity to walk through doors of opportunity. I was a far cry from my high school guidance counselor.

Dave was a living example to me of one degree. He risked on behalf of Lincoln to take a risk on me. He saw my need and potential and stepped forward to meet the one and unleash the other. It's like I've been saying, sometimes we're one person away from the help we need to receive and the hope we needed to give. The salvation I received was living, breathing proof of the power of my secret recipe. Looking into someone's life and sharing created an endless circle of fulfillment in my own heart—even when I was on the receiving end—and it would help me connect with those around me.

So, as I continued to work the deal in Nashville, I started a private, personal campaign that I called "Share the Love" where I would anonymously pick up the checks of men, women, families, anyone who looked like they needed some help in local diners and Waffle Houses. I would sit inconspicuously in the restaurant, wave down the waitstaff, and quietly pay for another person's bill before I slipped out unnoticed. At first, it was a little unusual for the folks waiting on the tables. They would ask, "Well, what should I tell them?" and I would simply reply, "Tell them they looked like they needed some love today."

I kept going back to the same places sharing the love, and the staff would get to know me. I still cherish the stories they would tell me about how people reacted and how grateful they would be. In pure dollar amounts, it was very little. Emotionally, though, it would brighten days, make people feel that there is hope and love out there. You should try it someday. It will give you such a high knowing you're doing something small and kind for your fellow man.

I could sense that there was something to this giving that I deeply enjoyed, something about it that seemed more significant than just a warm fuzzy for the day. But what that meant, I was unsure. And I didn't have too much time to find out at the moment. I had a deal to close.

4

An Old Self
Made New

The best way to get over any dysfunctions with money is to have very little of it. Though, I guess obsessing over the absence of a thing is similar to obsessing over an abundance of it. Still, when I had just a little bit of money, I had to form new patterns, new ideas. I had to see myself in a different way—not as a person who either had or didn't have possessions but as something entirely different and more human. Life had to be valuable on its own merit.

During my first month in the motorhome, I rediscovered the beauty of humanity, the loveliness of a smile lacking teeth, the grace of a limped walk, the purpose of a handshake. I rediscovered simplicity, and it was powerful. My heart still glows to think of all the nameless people, the momentary transients of warmth and generosity floating in and out of my life during that season. Sure, there were lonely moments, suffocating instants of self-pity, but those were eclipsed every day by passersby with shopping carts, moms in minivans passing me on the road, gas station attendants—our great neighbors of life. You have them, and I have them. Having nearly all my possessions liquidated, I could finally see that my fellow man was the purest treasure. And I was part of that hoard.

Yet, I couldn't take my affections and turn them into a tank of gas. I would still need actual money. So, while the Lincoln team worked through the purchase negotiations with the Nashville school, I was out crossing the United States calling on other prospects. I was gaping at the endless corn of Indiana, the demure beauty of the Blue Ridge Mountains. I got weepy at the mountaintops and worshipped with the rain.

One other simple treasure I had was the Walmart branded Rand McNally atlas with all of their Sam's Club and Walmart locations. Walmart has a policy that allows you to camp overnight in most parking lots unless it is against local regulations. They don't have hookups like a state park or anything, just a well lit parking lot with security cameras. And, of course, the sweeper vehicles with their low hum and soft scraping that would buff my plot of asphalt every morning at three o'clock. You might think that would become annoying. But it actually grew on me, a comfort of something familiar and expected. It was a huge snooze button. Once the sweepers came by, I knew I had three or four more hours of sleep left.

Contrary to popular belief, Walmart is not everywhere. So, as I wound my way through the landscape, circumscribing lakes, passing farmers' fields, and piercing mountains, I would sometimes treat myself to an official campground. And these were some of my favorite moments, when I'd roll in at dusk to a complex of nomads in RVs, backpackers in their sardine-can tents, children pedaling furiously on their bikes on the paved road looping through the numbered campsites. Campfires would be born on the forest floor as deck chairs unfolded. Husbands and wives and families, college kids and hippies and drifters would all recline in the first coolness of the day patrolling their forearms and calves for hungry mosquitoes. Beer cans would *plock* open and soothing conversations about life or *Seinfeld* or football would waft through the trees.

Yes, the campground is the Walmart of the wild, a soothing and assuring place that reminds you that people are the point of it all. TVs be damned, and marketing. Money can go the way of the dodo, so can keeping up with the Joneses. All you really need in life is a can opener. And maybe a fishing pole.

To Live You Need Breathe

Between July and September of 2002, I began to focus more on my health. I was working hard to redefine my mental illnesses, things like my hypervigilance that gave me unique capabilities. I was determined to redevelop any part of my past that could be helpful and harness it for the good. I would become the master of what had ruled me for fifty years and make it serve me and others positively. I had made much progress internally. But that was just the inside of me, the protein strands and gland secretions, the science of my old dysfunctions. Now it was time to give the exterior some touch-ups.

Many people with PTSD become alcoholics. Others, they like the drugs. And others still, sex. Me, I had a food compulsion, and I knew I needed to deal with it. I was morbidly obese and struggling with diabetes and self-image. Traveling across the country, I was a Jell-O mold behind the wheel. I waddled in and out of the motorhome, struggled with the hilarious smallness of gas station bathrooms and felt generally waterlogged all the time. I couldn't be healthy when fast-food marquees drew me in like a tractor beam. I could wax poetic about the unbelievable delicacy that is a French fry. I was determined for all that to change.

Thank You Al Roker

I had been waking up routinely with my friends on the *Today Show*. Al Roker was amazing me because he seemed to be sloughing off weight like a squeegee wipes away water. Then I remembered that he had a "vacation" a few months before. I suspected he had had weight loss surgery because he hadn't lost weight before, and they never talked about his weight loss on the show.

Several years back, I read about a surgery that would cause permanent weight loss. Even back then, just as I had experienced through my adult life, I had tried diet after diet. I would lose weight and regain it, somehow adding a few pounds every time in a yo-yo cycle of hope, success, failure, and pain. When you're addicted to food, you're constantly living like the Bible describes: "The things I do not want to do, I do. And the things I want to do, I don't." Translated for the food addict, it reads: "The donuts I should not want to eat, I do. And the carrots I should want to eat, I don't."

I truly, deeply wanted to be a carrot eater through and through. So, I feverishly thought about surgery. I scoured the

Internet, made phone calls, talked to fat people and skinny people, researched doctors and procedures, results and risks. I was chasing the dangling carrot and learning new words like *bariatric* and *metabolic* and *laparoscopic*. To make a long story short, it became clear that the permanent solution for me was this thing called laparoscopic gastric bypass surgery. Sounds lovely, right?

I had an important decision to make. My insurance company categorically declined my request for coverage of the surgery. One out of two hundred people die in surgery and others die due to some pretty common postsurgery complications. After all, if you are having this surgery your obesity is a serious health issue unto itself, not to mention the likely assortment of other health problems that stem from excessive weight. I had to sort out how much it would mean to my long-term health and wealth.

It was obvious even then that my weight and diabetes would ultimately lead to the "family badge," stroke, or death. With my family history of congenital disorders, this surgery was a lifeline, and no amount of money was too much when I considered the option between dying and living.

Here's the thing. I had just begun to turn around my finances after living several months dangling on a bankruptcy thread as thin as a silkworm's. The surgery and related expenses could cost as much as thirty thousand dollars, not to mention whatever it would cost for post-op care. Living in Walmart parking lots, you don't get the sense that a passerby with a full shopping cart will have an irresistible urge to wrap a stranger in some fresh gauze. I would have to get a hotel room for a couple of weeks and try to find some sort of help or recovery might be impossible if not deadly!

Summer quickly passed into fall, I was living off my Lincoln stipend, and I had resolved to undergo the surgery. The deal with the Nashville school was looking more and more certain, and I wanted to do the necessary research to find the right surgeon, the right place, and the right time.

Through my research, I had found a doctor in California who is internationally revered as a bariatric surgeon specializing in laparoscopic gastric bypass. His name is Dr. Alan Wittgrove, and he had pioneered the techniques and technology that he used in his top-tier practice. I spent hours and days studying his website, reading his case studies, living vicariously through the testimonials, and trying to stay honest about the risks.

I decided Dr. Wittgrove was the right surgeon, and the location of his practice, San Diego, was the right place to recover. My plan was simple: get in the door and on the list of patients with this world-renowned doctor. I had my endocrinologist and Dorney write letters of recommendation, I drafted my story, and sent them all to Dr. Wittgrove.

My cell phone rang a few days before Christmas.

"Hello?" I said into the phone curiously. Not many people were calling me those days.

"Paul Wittwer?" a gentle voice asked.

"Yes."

"Mr. Wittwer, this is Dr. Wittgrove calling from San Diego. I read your story and the letters from your doctors. I get letters from obese people all over the world, but tonight I was moved to tears. I want to be part of your life because I believe you are a winner. When can you come see me?"

My breath was missing as I choked back excitement.

"Dr. Wittgrove, I can be there as soon as your staff will see me. I have been preparing for this possibility for a long time." After a few initial tidbits of information and pleasantries, we ended the call. "Merry Christmas to you too," I said as the truest smile I've ever mustered painted across my face. I floated into the driver's seat of the motorhome and watched the hurried shoppers rushing in and out of Walmart.

The next day I began my preparations. I called Dave and tagged out of the Nashville talks temporarily, something I had already mentioned as a possibility. I reviewed my work with Dorney anticipating the psychological testing I would undergo for the pre-ops. I put every detail of a functioning life into place, in autopilot. I was about to descend into a deep but verdant valley of difficulty with the determination and intention of climbing the next mountain afterward. This time without being winded. I also want to say, because his kindness is so compelling, that Dave from Lincoln opted to continually pay my stipend while I was in surgery and recovery. That is the kind of person he is, one who shows the power of one-degree goodness.

MiniMe 2003

I've never been a New Year's resolution kind of guy. I mean, what for? Lose weight? Get married? Start some gimmick that flames and fizzles by February? I had given up on the myth of initiating new hope on a single day. I had learned in my Walmart life, though, that each new day needs a positive spin, needs to be seen as an adventure. If you have seen the Austin Powers movies, Dr. Evil created a clone of himself only it came out as a condensed version that he lovingly named "MiniMe." I was going to become a smaller version of me in 2003. A much smaller, healthier version. A me without one hundred pounds—my own MiniMe.

My pre-op consultation was January 27, 2003. Dr. Wittgrove's demeanor was calming and encouraging. We talked about my expectations of the surgery, his expectations of how I would honor this potentially lifesaving change, and what I hoped to gain as a result of it all. We spoke of my family heritage, the emotional and physical illnesses. I told him that if I had a good quality of life between ages fifty and sixty-five, then the risk and cost of the surgery would be well worth it. No one in my family had lived to see seventy, and none of them were healthy even into their fifties. He looked at me and told me that I was gaining an estimated twelve years just by having the surgery. He explained that obese white males lose twelve years off of their lives while obese black males lose twenty! My heart leapt with excitement. And my pocketbook was patting itself on the back—thirty grand for twelve years of better living is a pretty sweet deal.

Dr. Wittgrove used a dummy torso and the surgical apparatus to demonstrate the procedure. I sat there, five-feet-six weighing in at a whopping 265 pounds. My tree-trunk, forty-nine-inch waist and nineteen-inch tree-limb neck looked at each other with a smirk. They both knew that I was living a slow death by table fork. But the surgery would change all that or at least put me light years ahead in a new journey, the path toward MiniMe.

Life Is a Buffet

As a lifetime dieter, I had a solid track record of the "prediet binge." On Monday, you know you can't have Twinkies. So on Saturday you dine on them like a great white shark getting his fill on minnows. You're about to swear off steak so you worship at its beefy altar. Potato chips will vanish like the spores from dandelion weeds—you eat each one wishing it well for the future it must live without you.

But this surgery was no diet. Though my eating habits were about to drastically change, I couldn't do my standard gorge. It was the exact opposite. Prior to this surgery, your stomach needs to be as empty as possible. Preparing for the surgery was like a courtship with my soon-to-be life. I would learn for the first time what it meant to stare down a pastry and win. The hardest part was that I had to prepare for my own post-op life, which meant buying stores of "sick food" in advance, the Jell-Os and broths that get wheeled around your average hospital.

The day of my surgery, January 29th, I arrived at the hospital with my Fat Paul suit on. I waddled behind the nurse who took me to the prep room where a gown was waiting. It looked like someone had taken a curtain from a huge bay window and splayed it out on a clothesline. I undressed and looked at my belly, not knowing how to say all the things I had wanted to say. How it had been a good friend, how I was going to, in some way, miss it. I all the sudden felt bad for this part of me that had been the subject of so much scorn, discomfort, and dejection. It wasn't its fault, really. My belly stared back at me with a sullen look like it couldn't understand why I wanted to see my feet again. I stood in my small waiting room, the last blubbery statue of myself. And then there was a knock on the door. I quickly slipped on the gown.

In mere seconds I was on a gurney rolling down a sanitary corridor while masks and liquids and needles were moving in and out of my sight like a dance of an invisible puppeteer. My vision started getting blurry, lazy. I could feel my body fighting whatever was whispering a deep calm and blissful unconscious. But the drugs were too strong, and I succumbed. The next time I would open my eyes would be in a world full of vegetables and hope.

Surgery and Recovery

When you prepare for major surgery, certainly under general anesthesia, you worry about everything. Death during the surgery, irreversible complications, brain damage, and an endless list of "what ifs." Even when you have the world's best attending to you, the worry is still there. In my case I was on my own, no family or friends to see me on the other side so this had to go perfectly. I was prepped and ready to roll, IVs in neck and arms then lights out! The next thing I remember was beginning to wake up, I was in the recovery room.

My eyes opened slowly, and as I came to I realized I was struggling for air. For some reason I could not breathe through my nose. I felt as if I were choking, like being held under water and slowly drowning. I could feel death gripping me. I had been rendered unconscious before inadvertently through an accident, but this felt much worse, more fatal. I heard a voice coming from behind me. "Paul, just breathe, just breathe." My eyes were saucer-sized. My mouth was secured shut. I had a device protruding out the side of my lips but air would not pass through. Bright flashes of light started to cover everything— I was fighting for my life but I couldn't even move. I could feel the color of my skin turn a chalky blue.

Then the world started going fuzzy again. The surgeon's attendant suddenly realized my airway was blocked and hastily removed the restrictive device in my mouth. I coughed and spat up phlegm and saliva. I gasped for air that finally came. Once I was stabilized and breathing normally, I slipped back into unconsciousness.

Down the hall and through unopened doors, a Fat Paul suit was folded and laid on a back alley stoop for the trash man to pick up.

I next awoke in my recovery room on the bariatric floor, uncomfortable and challenged. I looked down over my body and there were so many tubes coming out of me I thought the doctor had accidentally sutured them in. Being in surgery reduces one to flesh and fluids. My lungs were laboring, and my blood was overloaded with sugar, then insulin shots. I had two intravenous tubes in my arms, a catheter, and two tubes coming out of my abdomen just below my rib cage—one connected to my old stomach and the other with a suction bulb to remove fluid from the internal surgical site. The long day bled into a long night. Doctor's orders, I had to forego my CPAP machine that helped me overcome sleep apnea, and I was constantly waking up, either from discomfort or the nursing staff with their annoying two-hour checkups, breathing treatments, and insulin shots. The day of my surgery would be the last day I would ever take medication for my previous Type II diabetes. My surgery has allowed me to keep my diabetes in remission through balanced nutrition, exercise, and discipline.

The rough night passed the baton to a rougher morning. Something was wrong. Dr. Wittgrove came into the room with a sense of urgency and ordered an emergency examination. Within minutes, a large glass of liquid chalk was shoved into my hand. I had to drink down barium the X-ray machine could detect, then I was taken to a room like a metal-reinforced bunker. The machine in the middle of the room looked alien. The X-ray was run and Wittgrove was hurriedly popping oversized photo negatives into a big light bar. I'm sitting there watching all this, half expecting them to inform me that an alien had snuck into my body or the doctor unknowingly lost his wristwatch during surgery. "Oh yes," I could hear Wittgrove saying in my mind with an alarming casualness, "there it is." I was afraid to glance over to see faint lettering R-o-l-e-x emerging from the fuzzy picture of my skeleton.

There was only slightly bad news. Evidently, my colon had been blown full of air sometime during the surgical preparation. Dr. Wittgrove smirked as he explained this all to me and said, "I don't want to be around when that comes out." The solution to this air pocket is a little too unsavory to share here. But let's just say it began with some invasiveness followed by extended walks through the hallways. Everyone made it a point to *not* stand behind me during the trips.

In the hospital on my own, there was no one to help me other than nurses. No visitors—just me and my helpers. Within a day and a half, some of the other patients were leaving with family. At the end of the third day after my surgery, I was the only person on the floor. Being alone on a hospital floor is eerie. The nurse's station was often unmanned, and the echoing corridors once filled with people felt like a hotel in its off-season lull. I didn't realize until they were gone how I had drawn strength and a distant camaraderie from the other patients and their families. The brief hellos and nods of wordless understanding were a significant connection for me. I would lie in bed browsing TV stations, a barely read book resting on the nearby nightstand. I decided to check out early. The fourth morning after my surgery, I gathered my stuff and called for a cab to pick me up. My post-op hotel room bunker with piles of Jell-O and cans of chicken broth was waiting for me. One person sent me flowers and a card while I was in the hospital, Dave Carney.

I was folding what few clothes I had when a bright-eyed nurse tapped on my door. She entered and was wearing a face of pride and hope for me, I could tell. It's an amazing thing to see someone's body language cheering you on. She was pushing in an oversized wheelchair, which, I gather, was a standard trick the nurses would pull. The scale of the chair made me feel less than tiny, like an infant in an oversized La-Z-Boy. Only it was no trick, the wheelchairs in the bariatric section are enormous because their patients are usually just the right size to fit them. When I sat in it, I already felt skinny. She rolled me through the halls, and I said my good-byes to the staff. I thought it would've been more emotional than it was. I wanted to grip each person in a bear hug. I wanted to gather what strength from them I could before leaving the safety of a place designed to help the weak. Who knew what would be waiting for me in the broad world?

The automatic double doors slid open, and the mild California winter wind was touching my skin, reviving my will to survive, succeed, and become the MiniMe I had envisioned days and years earlier. The cab driver was ahead of me in the driver's seat reading the paper mindlessly, passing the time until I maneuvered my way into the backseat. The nurse shut the door and about-faced with the wheelchair. It was just me, the cab driver, and an overwhelming fear that I was going to screw this up.

Walking and Talking with Lisa

I was on my own with my life in my hands. But I am an optimist, and I had a plan for my recovery. Prior to my surgery I had purchased a one-month bus pass for San Diego's transit system.

My strategy was simple. When I felt well enough to walk, I would get out of my room and begin walking the town. When I grew tired, I would get on a bus. I would repeat the cycle over and over to get my weight off as soon as possible. I started walking close to the motel the day after I was released and happened upon a small library close by. I marched myself in. Because I hadn't had access for days, I hopped on a computer to get online. I was curious to know what progress had been made in the deal for the Nashville school, was half hoping someone had written to check for me and my surgery. When I sat down, the lady in the seat next to me was scanning employment listings.

Talking to people out of the blue has become one of my favorite things. Having lived half my life without many solid, ongoing relationships, I've learned that you have to make friends in the moment, brief companions for life's journey. Sitting at that computer, I decided to start a conversation with my neighbor, and she told me she had lost her job. Her name was Lisa. She was a delightful, wide-eyed, optimistic thirty-five-year-old who had a zest for music, the environment, and personal health. I would learn that she had a penchant for administrative jobs and liked being responsible for the success of others. It was destined to be a perfect fit because I really needed the help. Besides, helping me gave her purpose while she was looking for work. For a Midwesterner like me, Lisa was the embodiment of the California girl—a free spirit willing to take the risk of new friendships while stuffing her car with recyclables for the next stop at the recycle center. I could not have been more fortunate than to randomly meet someone as personable, attractive, and kind as her in all of California. We found each other in a time of considerable need.

I went out on a limb with this perfect stranger and told her that I needed an assistant for a couple of weeks because I had just had surgery. She said I didn't look like I had had surgery, so I looked around to make sure no one was watching, pulled up my shirt slightly and showed her my tubes. I explained that I needed someone to check in on me and drive me around when I needed help. I offered one hundred dollars a day plus twenty dollars per diem for whatever she wanted. I would take care of each day's expenses, and each day I would pay in cash. My benefit to her was that she had cash money each day and a daily purpose to fulfill her gift of helping others succeed. This was my one degree commitment in motion—that I am one degree from someone I can inspire or who can inspire me, from someone I can help or who can help me. When you open yourself up to possibility, the possible finds you.

With the terms of our arrangement on the table, Lisa took a good, long look at me and agreed to do it. I guess she felt a fat guy with two tubes hanging out of his stomach wouldn't be much of a threat. And if he turned out to be, it wouldn't be hard to outrun him. We took a chance on one another.

In hindsight, I can't imagine those first days of my new life without her. Our first day, she took me to the historic Hotel Del Coronado. We had a wonderful meal together—her, salmon, me soup. I relished the interaction. We talked and ate and looked out to the Pacific Ocean. Over the next thirteen days, she was a wonderful companion and truly a godsend. I would wake up with my *Today Show* family, head out to walk the city, ride the bus, and meet Lisa whenever I needed help. I even went to the famous San Diego Zoo.

Part of the post-op plan was attending dietary counseling provided by the clinic. It was a group event with other patients who had had the same surgery in the previous week. I was shocked to hear people complain about how they were going to miss pizza, sweets, and all of the things that caused their troubles. I could hear failure in their whining. To succeed with this surgery, it was vital to think about all the things gained, not lost. Today, I can just look at a donut and feel queasy.

Good-bye Lisa, and Thanks

My two post-op weeks in San Diego passed quickly, and sadly it was time to say good-bye to Lisa and return to Kentucky and my motorhome. We stayed in touch through email over the following months. I would return to San Diego months later a much skinnier, healthier me. There was something about this woman that made me want to prove to her that I could get fit. She exuded a hope and encouragement, and I didn't want to let her down. When we met, Lisa was happy, in love with her then boyfriend, and employed. We eventually lost touch, but today I still look at the pictures taken of the two of us at the Del Coronado Hotel as we had lunch out by the ocean. I wonder whether I could have made it through my post-surgery transition without the one degree gift of finding Lisa, unemployed, sitting next to me at the library. Thank God I will never know what could have been without her perfect match to my need.

I flew back to Kentucky on February 12. Two days later, Valentine's Day, the transaction between Lincoln and NADC closed. Suddenly I was not only on course to becoming the MiniMe, I was also financially secure. As Dave told me on my birthday months ago sitting in the restaurant, I had earned a small fortune with the Nashville deal. In just ten months my income had gone from zero to more than five hundred thousand dollars.

But it wasn't because of me. Believing in one degree, showing love and care to the people around me, believing in myself, reshaping my illnesses, and trusting others had turned me around. When the news of the transaction came, my heart swelled with gratitude for Ann and Dorney. They had reached down into my life and pulled me up. I believed Dorney when he told me that if I did the work, I would have more peace of mind and more financial success than I ever imagined. I had survived the chaos! And I hadn't thought of my heirloom in months.

Citrus and Sunshine

Prior to the surgery, I had resolved to move to Florida once the Nashville deal went through. I chose Florida because there is no state income tax, lots of sunshine, and living there is an inland Midwesterner's dream. As soon as I felt able, I was on a flight to find my new home.

The first apartment complex I visited was Tuscany Bay in

northwest Tampa, which turned out to have on-site RV storage and they had a one bedroom first floor unit coming available April 1, in just two weeks. It sounded exactly right for the time being. I spent the rest of the week in a motel and organized plans for my apartment. Even though I had a lot of money now, I was still hesitant to spend it.

I signed a one-year lease, and my goal was to stabilize into a community, enjoy my new life, and become the slim, healthy MiniMe. It was strange and new to be on the upswing. I rode my bicycle, walked, used a YMCA and its community pool. Income from Lincoln had stopped with the closed deal in Nashville, but I had enough money for several years of modest apartment living, if not more. My entire focus became shaping a healthy body, adjusting to the restraints of my surgery, and redefining how I would live my life.

I started every day with a meal plan and exercise routine. My goals were simple and flexible. I wasn't driven to distraction by my obsessions, and my mind was never freer. In the first month after my surgery, I had walked off thirty-four pounds. My clothes size practically changed daily. I shopped at the Goodwill store to keep my wardrobe rotation affordable. My clothes didn't have to look great or be new; they just had to fit for a few weeks. When I changed sizes, I would take the large clothes back for a donation and buy something smaller. This went on for months.

Walking became a big part of every day. I had routes and mileages. Within two months I was able to walk up to ten miles in less than three hours. And this for a former fibromyalgia sufferer who couldn't walk more than ten minutes without hip pain in his past life. I also bought a new hybrid bicycle to cruise the miles of flat, extended paths around my neighborhood.

On the twenty-ninth of every month I would call the nurses who had cared for me on the sixth floor of the San Diego hospital. I would joyfully give them a report on my weight loss, status, and activities. Each week for the first month I also had a progress conference call with my post-op nurse in Dr. Wittgrove's office. She would quiz me on my eating habits and inquire about any problems. I knew my personal post-operative care regimen would also require local support. I was very fortunate to find Barbara Correll, a highly credentialed and certified nutritionist in Clearwater, Florida, who has worked with bariatric patients for more than thirty years. Her guidance in the early days of MiniMe helped me develop the bedrock direction and discipline to permanently succeed in my health quest.

It truly was the best summer of my life—freedom of mind, security, sunshine, and a *purpose*. As summer became fall, I reached my target weight loss. I had lost a total of ninety-seven pounds in nine months and weighed in at 167. I was free from diabetes, high cholesterol, triglycerides and blood pressure, fibromyalgia and joint pain. I had muscle definition from my forearms to calves. My abdomen had gone from a keg to a recognizable six pack. Best of all, I needed no cosmetic surgery. I was tight, toned, and ready to get back to work. I had control of my body, a positive self image and, along with my emotional conditioning, freedom from my food compulsion. Combined with peace of mind and financial freedom, the MiniMe was ready.

My waist size had reached a slim thirty-two inches. I had begun to shop for a totally new wardrobe, and a big department store was getting ready for a huge sale. I was going on a shopping spree—something I had never done before. I wondered whether I would even know how to shop for my new pipsqueak clothes instead of the XXLs I was used to buying. On my way to the mall, the air was charged with an excitement, a punctuation on all my progress.

Heading Out into a New World

While I enjoyed the summer, I still kept my ear to the ground for business opportunities and had sent out a couple of targeted mailings for new opportunities. On the last week of September, I decided to load up the motorhome and make a ten-day run to visit new prospects and start new business relationships. My first stop was Mooresville, North Carolina, where I visited another auto technical school and toured the facilities.

I then went to Wilmington, Delaware, to visit another school. Like I had learned in my Walmart life, wherever I went I found new adventures and stay active. What I mean is, I tried to get out where there would be people, places to be one degree from hope and help given or received, places where I could show love to people who seemed to need it. From Delaware I was off to Medina, Ohio, and then to Northbrook, Illinois. Each time I got on the road, I felt lighter. The roads rose to meet me while the horizon seemed easier to reach. The motorhome, my one place of familiarity through it all, seemed to run better. It had better pickup, a smoother ride, and I could sense the front grille turn upward into a smile every time I honked the horn pulling out of some parking lot. The coach had a musical horn with one hundred different songs, and I would swap them out to commemorate some national holiday or play a tune that the locals would love.

Knowing that life is a series of taking things on and letting things go, and despite all that it had been and meant to me, I decided that once this trip ended I would no longer make my business trips in the motorhome. I loved Kamp Kandu but it had been a symbol of my desperation and my salvation. It had delivered me and kept my head above water. I knew it was time to move on. It was time to lose such strong and conflicted symbolism.

When I crossed the Florida state line on the return trip, a tinge of sadness filled the cabin. I patted the steering wheel in a consoling way. And as I pulled into the drive of my apartment complex, I stayed in the driver's seat for a while reminiscing about all this machine had done for me. It was the cocoon of my transformation. As I killed the ignition, all the systems went silent. Every movement in the captain's chair reverberated down the long hull. I swiveled my head side to side like a camera panning in a movie taking in one final look of this, the last tour. I let the Walmart street sweepers roar in my ears as I looked at my grandmother's quilt folded in the corner. Al Roker was on the blank TV screen with a sad smile on his face. There was a sweet finality to it all, a chapter ending and a chapter beginning.

5

Fear Is Enemy
Number One

Fall turned to winter in the year of MiniMe. I had a great new wardrobe, a new car, and I was getting out of the apartment and mixing it up with the people. My goal was to establish a new life where friendship was possible, where people would want to be around me and undertake the great and mysterious transaction of relationship. Because I had finally reached the place in my weight loss where I thought I could get on the dating circuit, I joined a couple of singles groups and a business dinner club. I went on a single's cruise too. I didn't have the best track record dating, but I was determined to put my best foot forward. I was starting a great experiment to see if my internal healing could translate into external giving and vulnerability.

It was strange starting over at fifty-two, strange to be a toddler learning first steps. I would sit in cafés and restaurants and couldn't help but notice the beautiful servers and their cheery demeanor, their streaming hair and beaming smiles. For all I had accomplished in such a short period of time, there were plenty of relationship gaps. And like so many people who have, say, lost a spouse or a child, the holidays seem to have a particular knack at putting a finger right on the wound of absence. As Christmas approached, I was fortunate to have a colleague-turned-friend, Charles, invite me over for holiday festivities. He had season tickets for Orlando Magic basketball games and asked me to join him and his family to come along and share Christmas dinner with them. We cheered and laughed and taunted the referee just for the fun of it.

You never suspect how tall basketball players are, because on the court, when you're watching on TV, their height is all relative to one another. But in person, you get a better sense of their scale, which, suffice it to say, is absolutely ginormous. The game was a blast. And Charles's wife and two girls were the ultimate hostesses. I had been readily accepted and felt for the first time in a while that I could hold my own, that I could relate to people and ask them good questions, and laugh with the best of them.

After the game we headed back for Christmas dinner. Charlie and I were watching television and discussing business opportunities, including the potential sale of the company he represented. In that conversation, I shared some concerns about my own finances, especially estate planning. With my recent influx of cash, I knew I needed a good long-term plan. Charlie explained the use of a revocable trust for someone in my position with no heirs or family. He told me it is a powerful way to protect my assets and direct them to the destination of my choosing in the event of my death. Which, by the way, was still a sooner-rather-than-later possibility. I still had a ravaged family history of all manner of illnesses, any of which could find me at any moment. My long fuse hadn't completely flickered out somewhere on the long horizon.

He told me I could pick out a charity or institution I wanted to endow with my assets and enjoy helping them until I passed on. As Charlie was wrapping up his explanation— seriously, like it was a fated segue—a public service announcement came across the television for an organization called Give Kids the World, located in Kissimmee. The PSA was sponsored by Walmart. It turns out that Walmart was working to save more than the likes of me.

I was gripped by the images of hurting and terminally ill children laughing so unrestrainedly it seemed divine. It flooded into my heart and mind that just twelve months before I was dangling over a chasm and living in Walmart parking lots. And here I was trying to figure out how to bless others with my newfound wealth. The word *surreal* gets close to how I was feeling.

When I got home that night, I researched Give Kids the World and was moved to tears. Their mission and service aligned with many of the things I had experienced in my own life. It was like I had traveled to Orlando to be introduced to the revocable trust and hear that PSA in the same instant. A life drenched in selfless giving rushed on me, warm and raging, like a coastal wind.

I remembered my Waffle House ministry, and my heart lifted to think about sharing the love on a new scale. Giving unreservedly to others is like a soul salve that always sets me aright, keeps me centered in the true purpose of our time in this world. It was as if all of the months living in the Walmart parking lot were the proving ground for the theory of love. For the first time, I began to think about more than just living. I began to think about a giving legacy.

Growing Roots for Larger Branches

The day after Christmas, I began to seriously look for a house, and not just any house. I wanted to find the right place for me to grow. I needed the schoolhouse of life to give me a better education in living well. I was resolved to make the coming year my year of community. I found a good-sized but intimate home development where I could get grounded in my business and, hopefully, build meaningful relationships simultaneously.

Lamar Williams had finally decided to get serious about selling AMI, Inc. the motorcycle technical school Charlie represented. I created the necessary offering memorandum, contacted interested buyers, and we were off to the races to work a potential deal. With prospects in hand, and other prospective clients in the wings for my services, I finally felt secure enough to make a decision on a house. I looked for a place that would feel up to par with the houses around it and large enough to entertain. I knew that I would have to lure people into friendship with some dinners and parties. Because, and I say this without spite, people are so hard to get to know.

I was about to sell my motorhome, too, which had listlessly sat where I left it. The sale would go directly to the down payment of my new house, which was a beautiful way for me to end my era on the road and memorialize all the coach had done for me. The business relationships, trips, and life at Walmart that the motorhome ushered me to would ultimately earn more than two million dollars in income. It was a good friend indeed.

Emptiness Is an Invitation

The day I closed on my new house, I walked into its cavernous space and laid down on the living room floor. It was exactly twenty-three months from the time I sold my little house in Kentucky, just under two years of forced transience and uncertainty. I lay there not knowing whether to cry or to laugh or whether a distinction should be made between the two. It felt like my orbit had turned toward the sun.

In late April, just weeks after I closed on the house, I made it a priority to establish my revocable trust. I had found a good attorney through my realtor and was sitting in his office looking at the impression my house key was making in my jeans pocket. My eyes wandered to the coffee table where magazines had been artfully arranged, and I noticed a January issue of *People*. I mindlessly picked it up to pass the time.

If fate were a magician and this magazine its deck of cards, I was amazed by the trick. I ran my thumb over the edge of the pages and opened the magazine directly to an in-depth look at Give Kids the World. I couldn't believe it. Maybe it's just a contrivance or a half-truth, but I was compelled to see the world as something wonderfully and mysteriously interconnected, divinely interconnected even. I'm not sure what I expected to see, but I looked around the office like I was on a TV show that was orchestrating some powerful moment for me. As I read the article, I learned that the founder, a Mr. Landwirth, had survived World War II in his native Poland. He came to America with twenty dollars and built his life and wealth through the hotel business. His goal all along was to serve others. Now here was a story of triumph I could relate to. Everything within me wanted to emulate what I had seen in Landwirth—and to a similar, greater extent, Colonel Sanders.

I walked into the conference room where the attorney and some administrative staff were waiting for me and put down the magazine with a light thud. I opened it to the fated story I had just read. The attorney knew my personal story, how I had been homeless and floating toward the mouth of despair but was saved. I shared that I had no greater desire than to give to the world the salvation that was given to me. The attorney got misty-eyed. He said, "Paul, this life of yours is simply amazing." With a few more pleasantries and technicalities, I signed the document establishing my revocable trust endowing whatever wealth I would have upon my death to Give Kids the World. The *People* magazine had been in his lobby for four months awaiting my arrival.

A Three-Dollar Bill

Having bought a nice house and established a trust with my newfound wealth, you would think I had cleared a bar with money, that I had reached a healthy plateau. But I hadn't, and it deserves taking a moment to explain some things.

When my Dad told me he had all the money he needed to do the things he wanted before he killed himself, the truth is he had squirreled away quite a nest egg. And while that's okay, there is a strand of a story about money in my family that links back to my childhood, adolescence, and the constant struggle with money I saw in my Dad. As you'll learn, if you haven't already sensed it, I'm not too good with personal finances.

Watching my father's hard work for income spawned the entrepreneur in me. I started a lawn mowing service when I was eight years old, complete with a business card that read: "Paul's Lawn Service" with my slogan, "*Call Paul When Your Grass Gets Tall.*" When I was ten, my father showed me how to set up my first general ledger to keep track of income and expenses. At age eleven, I wanted to step up from a push mower to a lawn tractor and we found one used for nearly four hundred dollars. Dad took me to the bank and explained a signature note loan. It would be a loan for the entire amount under his signature and credit, but it would be my responsibility. He looked at me that day and in front of the banker said, "Son there are three things you protect all of your life: your credit, your character, and your relationship with your family."

Within three years, the fancy tractor went kaput, and I needed a new one. Three years after that, the second one died too. The bank became a Tractor Replenishment Center, and I was running my business solely on debt. By age thirteen, I had paid off the note on the first tractor but had a larger note on the second and was now responsible for a bank note totaling $905, an alarming sum for a teenager who's mainly concerned about avoiding acne. I had learned that borrowed money can buy you more impressive things faster. I also learned that when the first thing you buy gets all busted from use, you simply borrow more.

The same year I was wheeling and dealing with the bank, Dad took me to see a stockbroker. If you ever need a good laugh, try to explain the stock market to a careless country boy. You gotta love my Dad, though, in the hilarity. Here is a man trying to instill a responsibility and aptitude in me about the ways of the world. And what do I take away from it? That I get money for free. I learned that I could take my free money and invest it in companies that will make more free money on the money I just received.

As an adolescent, I became a regular poindexter. My mowing business looked like a bustling cottage industry to the unknowing onlooker. And I owned stock. Stock! I could toss around my success and get a little hit of dignity and praise. But little did my parents know—heck, little did I know—that I had cultivated an obsession. Making money and having stuff were the only means I knew to secure self-esteem. I had fashioned an admirable facade and used it to bolster myself, avoid people, and find a way to invest my energies.

In my growing-up years I developed a dysfunction with money that didn't go away by having plenty of it. Even though I had done considerable work with Dorney to reshape my

PTSD, the tensions with money were lurking just below the surface.

Building a Place for Friendship

But I did have a house, and I needed to get it ready for living. During my extended stay at the Walmart Astoria, I had dreamed of one day owning a home again. I dreamt of decorating it with musical instruments so guests could entertain one another. In my new home—I could see it in my mind's eye behind the wheel of the motorhome—I would have a large grand piano with an automated player system. So, the day my dream piano finally arrived, it was another out-of-body experience. I could hardly believe the drastic change that had taken place in my life. Another grand thing arrived, too, the check from the recent sale of AMI, Inc. It was just shy of half a million dollars with yet another hundred thousand dollars to come after the closing settlement. My banker, elated about the cash about to hit his vaults, went and picked up the check personally. But while this great boon was happening, something ominous was amassing. I say *ominous* because it was certainly a dark thing for me, though I would say that nature isn't quite as feeling as we wish it would be. The hurricane season was about to begin.

I had heard people talk about the power and devastation of hurricanes, but you can never understand their potential devastation and the resulting stress unless you live with them and through them. A hurricane by the name of Charley would be my first. It was roaring and whirling through the Caribbean and making its way to a seat of power in the Gulf of Mexico. The weather experts called for it to most likely turn back east and impact the state near Tampa Bay. They anticipated a Category 3 storm producing a surge of water thirteen feet high. Such a surge would have put my neighborhood under water.

I remember growing up in Kentucky where water was a blessed thing, something the old-timey farmers would talk about at the general store. People prayed for water, conjured it through age-old family superstitions. I had never been told, like I was hearing during Charley's rampage, that I should run away from water. To put this into perspective if you live inland or near the mountains, the average height above sea level in the Tampa area is only seventeen feet. A thirteen-foot storm surge would move the shore from the beach to your front door.

It's taken me some time to put a name on my fear. But it's clear to me now that hurricanes and the fear they cause was a clear trigger for my Post-Traumatic Stress Disorder. Imagining my home all soggy with me setting my ruined things out on the curb would send my heart and mind throttling downhill toward an insurmountable paranoia. And that's the difficult thing. This fear was legitimate, not a figment of my imagination. The fear preyed on me like a master tracker finding a wounded animal. Wherever I went, I left the stink of fear and a blood trail that could be sniffed out in the dead of night.

I knew the ravages of flooding. In 1997, my Kentucky home was wrecked by a flood that affected forty thousand homes in the Louisville area. I had to have assistance from FEMA and ultimately an SBA disaster assistance loan to remodel my wrecked home that put me upside down financially. Ultimately I lost thirteen years of equity in twenty-four hours. In part, the flood of 1997 and my financial losses that resulted from it put me in the Walmart parking lots. I knew firsthand the pain of placing all of my treasured, ruined belongings on the street for waste disposal. I was also injured during the flood falling down the basement stairs. And there I was living with hurricanes, it was terrifying.

I decided I had to get out of Tampa before Charley washed me away. I made some minor preparations and hopped into my Jeep. As I drove east to Daytona, my new house and all my new testimonies of improvement in my rearview mirror, I wondered what adventure was before me.

As I traveled, I monitored the storm through the small television in the dash of my Jeep. I watched in suspense as the radars showed this churning mass turn sharply eastward from the Gulf. Charley entered southern Florida in the Port Charlotte area and was headed across the state in a northeast trajectory that could include Daytona Beach. I was headed to Daytona myself and felt like a child too small to outrun the waves breaking on the beach. To this day, I swear I can see my fingers' indentations in the Jeep steering wheel from so many frantic miles.

Homeward

The storm passed while I waited it out due north. When I convinced myself I was intact, I headed home. All through the interstates, I passed cars like neighbors nodding in commiseration.

Even in the storm's most outward reaches, trees and power lines were down everywhere. Cars were parked unnaturally in ditches. Tattered and bedraggled families were carrying out rubble to the curb. And then I pulled into my driveway. I could hardly believe my eyes.

It was as pristine as the day I left it.

Like so many moments in my recent years, I wondered what all the worrying had been for, knowing that it had been for something. I had spent so much time and money toward the worthiest causes of my life—health and giving—and as a repayment I had hellhound hurricanes that would revisit me yearly. After Charley, I became afraid of Florida.

Within a few weeks, another hurricane came to us from the east. This time it was Frances, and the frightened masses expected her near Daytona where Lamar, my friend and the former owner of AMI lived. I called Lamar the moment I heard.

"Lamar, I just saw on the news you have a hurricane headed your way," I said trying to sound cool and collected.

"Yeah, we just saw that too."

"Are you and Patty going to evacuate?" Apparently for the Florida veterans, evacuating was more of an option than a necessity.

"We've talked about it and decided to stay. We're going to board up the windows and hunker down."

I'm sure my silence was suggestive.

"Why on earth would you stay?" I asked with a reprimand in my voice. "You live on the *beach*, Lamar." I was trying not to sound preachy, but I couldn't believe what I was hearing.

"We're gonna ride this one out. Everything is going to be okay. Besides, we don't feel good about taking our pets out of the house." I went ballistic on the other end.

"Lamar, that is absolutely ridiculous," I half-shouted into the receiver. "How could you put your life and your wife's life at risk like this?" He strung together some stats about how many hurricanes hadn't hit them though they'd seemed imminent, how evacuating was nothing but an inconvenience. Knowing there was no fight to win with him, I told him I would call after the storm had abated.

I'm not an I-told-you-so kind of guy. Three days later, I called and his roof had been torn off while they were in the house, which was now swimming in ocean swill. They were starting months of repairs while they continued to live in the house. The Florida heat plus the extended water damage bred invisible armies of mold, and Lamar got a severe respiratory infection.

The last time I saw him in June 2005, Lamar required oxygen to walk across the room. He was never healthy again after the storm and died in January 2006 at age sixty-two. Lamar's tragic and untimely death was mortar for my fears. I equated a blasé attitude with certain harm—and I attributed it all to the hurricanes. I began to question my decision to move to a state where nature could, at a moment's notice and with annual certitude, trigger my mental illnesses.

Some of my financial health was tied up in my home, which could become mere fodder for a storm and detritus for the outgoing waves. Looking back, I wish I would've left. In a life of one degrees, though, things happen for a reason . . . including this.

Tony

Late July, I was generally worrying about hurricanes and plotting how to build community when a text message appeared on my cell phone from Verizon. It read, "Your service in Westchase has been improved, for more information press star then 68." I had never received a text message, so I thought this was a gimmick to add more to my bill. I quickly deleted it. Two weeks later it appeared again, the same message. *Persistent devils*, I thought. *Now they are going to hound me until I give in and pay more for something I don't need.* I deleted the message again. The following week, the same message twice. I was annoyed, so I decided to go to the Verizon store and find out what the message was all about and how I could stop it.

When I walked into Verizon, there was a sign-in sheet full of names yet to be served, so I put mine on the list and sat down beside a Hispanic guy who I would guess was ten or fifteen years younger.

"How long you been here?" I asked.

"Two hours," he sullenly replied in broken English.

"Wow! I wonder what's taking so long," I said out loud and to myself. "What are you here for?" I asked.

"I dropped my cell phone and it broke. But I didn't have the insurance, so now I must replace it. My father-in-law gave his old phone, but it doesn't work on Verizon's service." He said all this gazing down at a mangled thing that could've been a phone once. In the other hand was the father-in-law's donation. I think I saw him begin to tear up.

Now, I realize a broken phone is a sad thing, but not that sad. I sensed there was a deeper story behind his visit to the store. I introduced myself with a handshake, and he said his name was Tony. I politely asked him to tell me about himself. He said he had to have a phone because it was his lifeline. Without the phone he could not keep up with his two children, work at his job, and keep up with the needs of his wife who was in the hospital. I asked why his wife was in the hospital.

"Mr. Paul," he said, "two years ago my wife did a breast self-examination and felt a small lump. She had just gotten a job at Walmart and was not on the insurance plan for another two months. When she was covered, she went to the doctor because the lump had grown, and after a lot of tests, they determined that she had breast cancer and gave her six months to two years to live. Mr. Paul, it has been two years and my phone is the only thing that keeps me from going crazy. I don't know what I am going to do because I simply don't have two hundred dollars to spend on a phone." He paused with the gravity of broken hope.

"Somehow, Mr. Paul," Tony rebounded, "I know the Lord is going to see me through this. I just know he will."

I instantly knew who had been sending me the text message, and it was not Verizon. I looked at Tony and said, "The Lord sent me here today to take care of your phone needs." The way Tony looked at me, I wondered if a strange aura of light burst out behind me, but realized I was sitting in front of a powerfully lit marketing display. Tony looked at me puzzled and started to ask why when a store attendant walked out with "There's nothing we can do" written all over his face. The attendant told Tony what he already knew about the father-in-law's phone. I interjected and told Tony that I was going to buy his new phone. He jumped from his seat.

I told him about how I kept receiving the strangest text message, and that I was visiting the store to get it to stop. But having heard his story, I told Tony I believed I was sent there to be at that Verizon store, that the Lord had blessed me with some money, and I was there to help his family. I looked at the attendant, who had been standing there dopily, and asked him to recommend a replacement phone. He came back with the model I was using, and I already had the money in hand. Then Tony started to cry. And I did too.

The Verizon worker, having heard most of this strange transaction, got his manager to approve a forty dollar discount. And I smirked at Tony as I requested the monthly phone insurance. I said, "If you drop it again, it will be the insurance—not the Lord—that will replace it." There was also a thirty dollar rebate I requested be sent to Tony to help him with his bills. Tony asked for a business card. I looked at him and said, "No, if I give you my card, you might want to pay me back someday, and I won't accept it." I just gave him my cell number and asked him to keep me informed about his wife and family. He pulled a card from his wallet, and on it he wrote his name and his wife's and his cell phone number. The business card he gave me was from the hospice nurse assisting his family.

We walked out of the store together. I never talked to a representative about the text message. I didn't need to—I knew who sent it. Strangely, it never came to my phone again after Tony.

The Great Spiral

Though I was desperate to leave the state because the hurricanes were unraveling me, it had become the only place of stability I had known in my "new life." Westchase and the few neighbors I had built relationships with were my only family. But after Katrina and Rita in August and September, I felt I had too much tied up in my oversized home. I hatched a plan to downsize to a more modest neighborhood nearby. The good thing was, my home had appreciated dramatically in just sixteen months. The market was hot for big homes, and they moved quickly, so I was glib about the likelihood it would sell.

In September, I started step one. I bought a golf course villa home and began to remodel it immediately. Even though it was only three years old, it felt cheap from stock finishes. I was confident that I could temporarily straddle two mortgages and sell the big house as soon as possible.

During this, my cell phone rang one day with a number I didn't recognize. I answered, and a delightful voice said, "Hello, Mr. Paul. This is Tony. We met at the Verizon store!" A month had passed since the day I bought him a phone. He was thanking me for what the phone had meant to him and his family while hospital paging blared in the background. Solemnly, he shared that they were preparing to disconnect life support and that his wife was expected to pass in two days. I asked about his children and how everyone was doing. He choked back tears. We spoke for a few more minutes, and in closing the call I asked him to call me when his wife passed, if he could.

Three days passed, and I got a call on my cell from a number I now recognized. It was Tony. I answered, and a female voice identified herself as Tony's sister, and she was calling to inform me that Tony's wife had died. She asked how I knew her brother. I told her simply that we had met at the Verizon store and nothing more. We exchanged a few more words, she told of the memorial service that I couldn't attend due to business travel. The story about Tony, his wife, and my distant inclusion came to a sobering close.

Early in 2006, the value of my first home had grown from just over half a million to just under a full million. I was so proud of my investment growth that I turned down an offer that would net more than a quarter million in profit. It was the stupidest thing I had done in a long time. I just couldn't see what was headed my way.

If I could've, I would have shed myself of some heartache long before it became misery. For, in the short months between resolving to downsize and actually doing it, the housing market started to take an aggressive downturn. At first I shrugged it off—I had great cash reserves and the market had been stable for so long. Plus, I wanted to recoup as much of my remodeling cost in the smaller home in the sale of the bigger one because those costs were ballooning. And so was—I have to admit now in hindsight—my ego from financial success.

Trying to Find a Home

By January 2006, I had the big house on the market for sale by owner with a price in the $900,000s. I was overly optimistic and stress began to set in as the market for large homes shrank and my spending on the villa grew. Weeks crawled into months, and the months seemed like years. By March it was apparent the market was stalling, if not collapsing. I also began to realize that I had made a mistake in choosing the neighborhood of the golf villa. This one had a Homeowners Association that was rife with "condo Nazis," the people who get in your face and complain about everything you do, right or wrong.

The business trip I had to take rather than attend the wake for Tony's wife turned out to be the largest completed sale I would initiate for Dave's company, Lincoln, the one based in New Jersey. There were seven companies trying to acquire the same school, but I was able to get in the door and help my clients persevere to close the deal for tens of millions. My reduced fee was still just a fraction of that, a good deal for my good friends who had saved my life. This happened just days before my fifty-fourth birthday, and my mind instantly went back to Dorney and what he said, that if I would do the work, I would have more financial success and peace of mind than I had ever known.

The financial success part of the equation proved more doable than the peace part. The choices I had made to live in Florida and then attempt a complicated transfer from my first house to the second were robbing me of peace. Further, the villa was robbing me of my cash and the market was robbing me of my big home's value. I began wondering if I shouldn't just cut my losses and leave entirely. Then I saw this crazy-scary report on climate change and the effect it would have on coastal areas. Florida was featured and a scientist walked viewers through a not-too-outlandish hypothetical scenario where my home could be covered by the sea. For me, that was it. If a scientist on TV could trigger such fear in me, regardless of the legitimacy, I knew I had to leave. Perception can be reality, and I perceived that I could not be happy in Florida.

The year before, I had developed and completed an acquisition opportunity of a cosmetology school in Las Vegas for Dave's Lincoln Educational Services. In researching the cosmetology school industry, I had become friends with Jim Cox, the executive director of the American Association of Cosmetology Schools based in Scottsdale, Arizona. I recalled the small endorsements he had made for Arizona as a retirement state. I wanted to trade my drenchable, sea-level stress pool for high desert. He suggested Prescott, Arizona.

Prescott is the kind of place you can fall in love with quickly, certainly if your roots are in rural life. First of all, it's nearly a mile above the sea. And its harsher seasons are quite mild. The population feels like an embellished township full of baby boomers and Republicans. Prescott is always ranked in the top ten places to retire. Even though there are two Walmarts in the area, the downtown square thrives. And for good measure, it is the birthplace to the American rodeo, though I hear this is hotly contested in quarterlies and local newspapers up and down the foothills of the Rockies.

Prescott, yes, was my kind of town, and I wanted to be there as soon as I could. I redoubled my determination to leave Florida. But the market kept slipping, and I went into the fall of 2006 paying two mortgages. I moved most of my furniture into the villa to stage it for potential buyers. It left my actual house strangely empty and echoic.

Simplifying When I Can

As the housing market eroded and my desire to leave strengthened, I had a strong drive to simplify. An easy target was this luxury car I had. I was more comfortable in the solid metal and stiff shocks in the trucks of my childhood memories. For nearly three decades, I had wanted a 1951 Ford pickup like the one my dad owned. Perhaps I wanted to insert some familiarity into the madness or coerce the redemption of a memory.

I found one on the Internet that was almost exactly like the one we had in our family for so many years. I called a friend of mine in Detroit, Mike Stewart, who had retired from Detroit Diesel and now worked for Lincoln. He had more than thirty years of hands-on experience restoring vintage vehicles, and I asked him to take an adventure with me to see the truck. I flew into Detroit, and together we drove to a northern

Indiana farm where the truck had been gracing the big barn. It was waiting for us at the end of a long gravel road. Even from a distance, I knew.

Mike was talking all the while, but I didn't hear him. With his expert's seal of approval and with my childhood swimming in my head, I made an offer and bought the truck. It wasn't a toy or even a vehicle really—it was iron and glass and memories. Many an evening I would flip on the garage light just to gaze upon it and get lost in the unmistakable smell of a childhood lifetimes away.

—

A few days after I bought the truck, the seller sent the title express mail, which required my signature. Our postal carrier, Maria Wilson, rang the doorbell and handed me the envelope. It was rare that we would talk to one another, and as I signed her clipboard, she looked over my shoulder into my house.

"Is that a seven-foot grand piano?" she said.

"No, it is a six-foot-eleven-inch concert grand."

Most folks don't know what kind of piano they're looking at. In my family, music, especially pianos, had been a staple for entertainment. I have an upright Adler player piano that has been in my family since Christmas Day 1915. I have been playing and singing with it since I was eighteen months old. After my parents' death I had it restored and collected more than seven hundred music rolls. That my postal carrier had an eye to recognize the grand, the other newer piano I had, made me curious. I invited her to take a look. As it turned out,

Maria was a classically trained pianist who had taught piano for twenty-five years. She sat down on the bench in her unflattering US Postal uniform, cracked her fingers, and played works by Chopin, Handel, Liszt, and Bach. She transformed into something fiery and unbound. Her carrier bag was still strapped crosswise over her torso. We then went into another room where the old player sat; Maria rattled its keys with ragtime tunes, one-steps, and blues.

After about thirty minutes, with her truck still idling in my driveway, Maria snapped to and declared she needed to get back to work. It was like the Muse of music knew she had responsibilities to keep and extracted itself, floating on to find the next unwitting soul who would have the joy of creating beauty. Maria collected herself, straightened her hair, and lightly grazed the keys with her fingers one last time as she rose from the bench. Near the door, I told her I was going to start sending myself Express Mail so she would come back and play for me.

———

I think I caught a Muse too. With a 1951 Ford in my garage, I became somewhat obsessed with the truck and thought to get another. Perhaps I would become a collector. I began researching car collecting feverishly and learned it's best to focus on a year, identify the best and rarest models, and attain them one at a time as fully restored as possible. Within months, I found one that fit the bill. In Buffalo, New York there was a very rare extra cab model in the even rarer alpine blue. It was a solid restoration. I flew to Buffalo, bought the truck, and had it shipped to Tampa.

And along came Maria with my papers.

———

On the day I saw Maria again, I thought back to her performance and wondered how many people in the neighborhood had any clue that this modest virtuoso was using her lithe fingers to lower mailbox flags. I wondered how many people had even thanked her for her simple service. Then I got a flash of an idea: a "Maria Wilson Surprise Appreciation Party."

As I signed the papers for the truck title, I told her that I was going to invite some neighbors over, and I wanted to know if she would come over and play piano for the party. She was so excited, talked to her husband that night, and accepted the offer. From there, I made up an invitation to the secret Maria Wilson Surprise Appreciation party and mailed it to forty of my neighbors, all of whom she served in the postal truck. The invitation explained her talent and gift of music. A couple of days later, Maria sent me an email and wanted to know if her eighty-year-old mother, Rose, could come too.

The night arrived, and so did forty guests, Maria, her husband, and her mother. Thirty minutes into the evening, I asked Maria to play for us as we all gathered around the piano in the living room. She was spectacular as she had prepared a concert and seminar on the life and music of Chopin.

After her second song and Chopin history interlude, I interjected with an announcement. I told her that her invitation was different from everyone else's. Along with a delicate, gold treble clef charm, I handed her what all the other guests had received while we all waited in anticipation. Maria sat there stunned, and she handed the invitation to her mother. Tears and smiles began to form on both of them, and the whole room clapped riotously. There was something intoxicating there, something irresistible, and it had to be applauded. Maybe it was simple human connection or taking the time to praise an individual who often lives overlooked. Or it could've been that each of us saw a piece of our own hidden glory, and clapping for Maria meant clapping for ourselves too.

The next day she called me, still overwhelmed that someone had done so much for her. I could hear her thumbing the gold charm I gave her to commemorate her evening. She said she had been with the post office for thirty-three years and rarely had a customer even said thank you.

6

The Purpose of
One Man's Life

PART ONE

I basked in memories of the Maria party for at least a week. It felt unspeakably good to have brought surprise to her life and joy to the lives of my neighbors. I don't think it was my imagination, but I could tell people felt more connected to Maria after that. And I hoped they thought differently, too, about anyone who goes overlooked in life. Since the party, I had constantly reevaluated the where, how, and why of life. Experiencing true joy will do that to you, make you step back and question whether you deserve a bit more of it.

My noble plans of building community and taking the next step forward in my healing hadn't gone quite as I'd hoped, though. Further, my trucks, though a great testimony to the loving years I had with my Dad, were punctuation marks on the lack of people in my life. I was rightfully proud of my incredible and unlikely turnaround. I went from dangling over bankruptcy by a silkworm thread to being a millionaire. And yet, my heart was not full. *Why?* I would ask myself over and over. See, accomplishment was new to me. So why was I not complete? Why couldn't I come to grips with success?

Saved by Pie

Ten days after Maria's party, I was on one of my listless walks in the house, wearing tracks in the carpet like an aimless beast. This inward tendency to stay by myself was exactly why I had pasted on my computer "Get out of the house once a week." Interacting with other people, especially finding a way to do something special for them, was the foolproof curative for my malaise.

It was on this day that hope came to me instead of me going to find it. By now, because of parties, most of my neighbors had been in my home. Virtually all of them had children. When they were at the house, I made a point of telling all the parents that if their children were ever selling things, please send them to my door. I wanted to see how the children would present their product or service, maybe give them some pointer or inspiration, and I would certainly buy whatever they were selling, even if it was useless.

My doorbell rang. I opened the door to a neighbor and her two daughters selling things to raise money and support for their school causes. The first one began her presentation—she was selling ten dollar gift certificates for homemade pies from the Village Inn restaurant. She explained how the money would be used and how much money her class needed to raise. Her presentation was sincere and convincing. After gastric bypass, I could not eat pies or sweets, but she didn't need to know that. I went into my office and brought out a check for one hundred dollars to buy ten certificates. Her eyes bulged out of her head, and she looked up unbelievingly at her mom. I put a stop to the "Paul, you didn't have to do that" and all the other expressions of sincere and contrite thanks. And in all the commotion of gratitude, the mom happened to glance in and see the concert grand piano and remarked on it.

Seizing the opportunity to get jolted out of my carpet-treading funk, I asked the children if they would like to see the instruments that they could just spy in my living room. Maybe they felt obliged because I had just bought one hundred dollars' worth of inedible pies, but it didn't matter. Little did I know a divine appointment was just a few minutes away.

I walked them through, highlighting and briefly explaining all the musical instruments, including the room that had my 1915 player piano and the seven hundred rolls of automated music from 1900 to present. The room was decorated with pictures from my childhood when I had my lawn service and my vision board that I made when I was eighteen years old in 1970. It is a decoupage of various things I had enjoyed in my life up to age eighteen and things I wanted to enjoy or experience in the future. It has images from various sources, photographs, my first business cards, ends of a piano roll box and so much more. In the middle of the board is a picture of a Harley-Davidson motorcycle torn from a sales brochure. I stopped at the vision board and soap-boxed on why it's important to have a dream and a goal. I looked at the girls and said while pointing to the year 1970 in the left-hand corner, "Can you imagine that I constructed my vision board in 1970 and thirty-four years later I represented the sale of the American Motorcycle Institute and earned over a five hundred thousand dollar commission?" Their eyes went as wide as saucers! And I told them that what they were doing that day raising charitable funds was great practice for a fulfilling life. My vision board hangs in my office as I write.

They smiled politely, and as we made our way to the front door after the abbreviated walk through my past, the older daughter looked at me and said, "Mr. Paul, you did not ask about what I am offering today." She had a pouty face that would make me grab my checkbook, of that I was sure. I asked what she had to offer, and she told me her high school class was raising money to help the children hurt by Hurricanes Katrina and Rita. She handed me a pamphlet explaining the charity. As I scanned it, tears welled up in the bowls of my eyes. It was quite uncomfortable for us all, I admit. And I didn't mean to put this beautiful trio in a weird spot. But when the mother asked me what was wrong, I simply handed the pamphlet to her and pointed at the small headline, "Help Children Recover from Post-Traumatic Stress Disorder."

The Purpose of My Life

As they stood there, it was as if a reel of my past overran my field of vision. Images of Billy and my prepubescent self, my guidance counselor, and my heirloom were all crowding my head like a mob elbowing their way to the front of a line. I kept trying to peer around them to keep eye contact with the mom and her girls, kept trying to hold back my emotions.

I pulled myself together as best as I was able and explained that I had been challenged by PTSD all my life, that I had been diagnosed with and had begun to manage the illness when I was fifty years old, became homeless, and rebounded to the level that they now saw. With my face wet and puffy, I wrote out a check for one hundred dollars to keep things equal and emphasized how important her effort can be to those children we would never meet. I wanted to give so much more.

I had no doubt in my mind that God had brought this moment to my door. And it was the instant that everything changed, the instant when I understood my life's purpose.

—

Ann, Dorney, the unexplained text message that brought Tony into my life, Maria, my neighbors, the fund-raising youngsters. One degree from hope and help. One degree. I was always one degree from someone whose life I could influence or who could influence mine. As the door closed on my visitors, I wept for the children I would never meet, for the pain they would know as I had known all my life.

—

The following afternoon, I received a call from the mother.

"Paul," she said excitedly, "you lit a fire under my girls like you would not believe. They came home and started practicing their piano so they can put on a recital for you. Thank you so much for sharing your story and walking us through your home."

The call lifted my spirits, though I was still groggy from what had happened the day before. I didn't have enough puzzle pieces to understand why I had felt the way I did when I gave even just one hundred dollars. It felt like a small redemption, that what had been taken from me because of my illnesses could be fought for others. I had never felt like that before.

Two days later, the Mom called again and told me her girls wanted to know if I could participate in the Great American Teach-In. She explained that the Teach-In was a day when adults went into a classroom and gave a lesson or story of their choice. One of the girls had suggested that I would be perfect to talk to the sixth grade orchestra class because of my love of music and my instrument collection. I asked what I would be expected to talk about and she said anything of interest and maybe my musical instruments. I accepted the invitation almost immediately not really knowing why. In fact, everything within me was telling me no, but it was the kind of internal no that was easily trumped by some greater, noble compulsion that I couldn't resist.

I was to show up on the Thursday before Thanksgiving and talk to two different classes for thirty minutes. Permit me a moment to confirm the anecdotal statistic that Americans fear speaking more than death. The proposition of talking in front of people raised my hackles much more than the thought of suicide ever had.

I had less than a week to prepare. Then it hit me—why not give a lesson based on my life and how I had once sat in their seats? Why not inspire them with change, challenge, and overcoming? That hope and help were just an arm's reach away if they would but reach for it? Yes, this was the presentation that made my heart come alive. With days to go, I titled my presentation "Imagine Your Possibilities: What Matters Most Is How You See Yourself."

On the day of the Teach-In, I arrived early with my hands full of instrument cases and a duffel bag. The middle school had a check-in area for guests, and I walked in nervously. I used to sweat a lot when I was fat. As MiniMe I didn't sweat much. The day I walked into the middle school, I was a water hose.

I was approached by one of the teachers, we made brief introductions, and headed to the orchestra room where I met the music teacher. She told me about the class and the orchestra program as I unloaded my bag of props and uncased the musical instruments. I wrote my name on the blackboard, "Mr. Paul." As the class filed in, I got the once-over from all the children. The teacher went through her usual routine and got the class seated. Then she introduced me, "Class, this is Mr. Paul. Please say good morning." The class responded in unison with a hearty "Good morning, Mr. Paul." And then they stared. And I stared. There was lots of staring. And then I realized they were waiting on me to begin.

"Today friends," I began nervously, feeling my heart rate quicken, "I want to inspire you to imagine your possibilities.

I want you to understand that what matters most is how you see yourself.

"I would like to tell you a story of overcoming in my life, and how people, especially teachers," I said as I motioned in the teacher's direction with a knowing smile, "have helped me. Or hurt me. And how there is always hope and help if you only ask." The looks on their faces told me this was not going to be a normal class day for them.

"As I share my life with you, I ask that you pay close attention. Even though I'm much older than you, I once sat in a chair like the ones you're sitting in today. I once walked through school hallways and experienced the same things you experience. In some parts of my story, you may recognize a bit of yourselves. Parts of this story I hope you never experience." I had their attention, and with that I took a small balloon from my bag that was already inflated.

I held up the balloon and began to squeeze as I told them about growing up fat. I told them about the beginnings of some medical illnesses that were rooted in changes and happenings out of my control, like moving to a new house or getting into fights at school. All the while the balloon stretched nearly to bursting. The kids held their ears waiting for the pop. I explained that life was just like the pressure on the balloon. Pressures from our parents or siblings or an upcoming test compress the balloon. While we are trying to handle those pressures, other parts of the balloon grow weak and can cause the balloon to pop. When we try to address the weak parts of the balloon, then the other points of pressure need equal attention.

I admitted that life can feel confusing at times when we don't understand the different pressures or how we can handle them. I then held the balloon in the air with a single hand stating, "The only time your balloon will be perfectly round without pressure is when you are in your mother's womb and for some of us not even then."

I went on to tell them about my third grade teacher, Mrs. Benson, who saw something special in me, passing another mirthful glance to the teacher. Mrs. Benson discovered that I could sing and made me the daily class song leader. Her encouragement gave me the confidence to attend school regularly where my attendance had been very poor and troubled in my first two years. I spoke of self-image and weight issues. I told them about my guidance counselor, making the contrast between the two teachers and their impact on my life. I could almost see the parents in attendance leaning in at this point too. In a sense, I was a poster child for the impact an adult can have on a child for good or for ill.

I took from my bag a half-filled bottle of red Gatorade with the label off. I held it in front of me and began to rotate it end over end slowly and asked the class what they saw. One boy said, "Mr. Paul, the liquid is not sticking to the sides." "Right," I said. "It is not sticking to the sides because it is seeking its own level. The fluid is finding its place where it is most comfortable." I explained that a teacher I once had made me feel stupid in front of other kids. As a consequence, I began to see myself as stupid. I believed that I could achieve little. I believed that because my brother was smart and accomplished in school, I must be the dumb one, and just like the Gatorade, I began to gravitate to the level where I thought I belonged.

"It is that personal image of *you* that determines how others see you too," I said with conviction.

I knew I was laying some heavy stuff on the kids and that maybe I should tone things down. But something deeper, that deeper yes, pushed me forward. For some reason, I *needed* to share this and they needed to hear it. Talking to kids like they're adults every once in a while makes them feel bold and mature, like they have a seat at your table.

Being mindful of the time, I whisked through a couple more maxims. For instance, I held up two B-flat trumpets, one a small pocket trumpet and the other a regular full-size, explaining that though these were two different-sized instruments they sounded exactly the same because they each had the same length of tubing. "Within each of us," I said translating the metaphor, "we all have the same length of tubing. The only difference is how we *choose* to toot our own horn."

I quickly relayed my post-collegiate experiences, my successes, my IQ revelation, and my revitalized perspective. But then, I came to the truly difficult part. My suicide attempt. And don't worry, I didn't tell them about it. They were too young to understand, and I didn't want to freak them or the parents out.

But I did tell them that when I was forty-nine years old, I was diagnosed with an illness, and to manage that illness I wound up homeless, diabetic, and obese, living in Walmart parking lots. The room was dead silent for a moment. Then a lone hand slowly raised in the back of the room like a thermometer that finally gets to a final reading. "Mr. Paul, what kind of illness did you have?" I looked at the teacher as if to say, *I'm sorry if this causes you too much trouble afterward,* took a deep breath, and said, "Young man, I had a mental illness, an illness that is known as Post-Traumatic Stress Disorder, PTSD." The teacher interjected how it is an illness suffered by war veterans and victims of abuse. The young man raised his hand again, "Mr. Paul, do you still have it?" I replied, "Yes I do, but I have learned to manage my challenge and that is why I can be here with you today."

I turned to my prop table again to change the momentum in a positive direction and pointed to a metal gong on its stand. It had the name Zildjian branded across it. I began to tell the history of Zildjian, an Armenian alchemist in the city of Constantinople in the seventeenth century who had developed a special metal that gave their cymbals a great sound and sustain. I hit the gong, and everyone shuffled in their chairs with smiles. I told them how this man had identified *the one thing* he could do very well, and his namesake has continued to this day making the best cymbals in the world.

My point, I told their confused faces, was that I came into a new life, that I had discovered one thing that helped me to become the person who stood before them: how I saw myself determined who I would become. I enthusiastically told them that no matter their size, what their teachers told them, or what they felt capable of, each of them must discover for themselves that one thing. "And that," I said like

Tony Robbins as I went to my prop bag, "starts with personal vision and imagining your possibilities!"

I pulled out a cute picture of a kitten looking into a mirror and looking back at it was a lion. Above the drawing there was a phrase, "What Matters Most Is How You See Yourself." I had a picture for each of the students. I asked them to place it somewhere they would see it every day for a week. And if after that week they did not believe it, then they should keep looking at it until they did. "Maybe until you are fifty years old as I had to." It was laminated to withstand grime, slime, and time. With an awkward smile, I closed and said thank you.

The teacher said a few words, and as the class dismissed, she came up to me with tears in her eyes. I just knew I'd done something wrong and upset her. But quite the opposite, she told me that I had given her hope for her son who was bipolar and schizophrenic.

Buying things from my neighbors had put me one degree from someone who needed hope and help. I packed my bag of props, and as I left I reassured the teacher that there was always, always hope and help.

—

I went home exhausted. The tension of reliving and telling my story in front of children and strangers had worn me out. When I got home, I sat my bag down and stood in the living room seeing the faces of the children like a class photo. I had never revealed myself to an audience. I walked out into the garage and stared at my old Ford trucks while the gravity of what I had done settled in on me. I had brought inspiration to one teacher and possibly spoke a life-changing truth into the lives of those children.

I walked around the trucks thinking about the day when they were new in 1951 and how many loads and miles they had seen in their lifetimes. I thought about how my generation would be the last to see the old trucks as they had once been, not as collections in a vintage show but as the workhorses they were bred to be. I thought about all of the people who were like me with vintage vehicles sitting in their garages, rarely driven, life stories sitting around wasting precious time.

Perhaps it was the smell of the trucks that always conjured memories of my dad and my growing up, a yearbook of all my trials and my unlikely turnaround. Perhaps it was how those smells and memories related to my experience that morning. But as I stood on the stoop of my garage surveying life, I realized I had a choice. And that choice hit me like a shockwave that nearly knocked me over. I could either be a dusty old truck, good for nothing but nostalgia, or I could be a workhorse for the good of others.

It sounds a little odd looking back, but the determinations to make an impact for the good evolved into, *What if I could start an organization that would get people to take their vintage vehicles and their life stories to schools and share the "one" thing that helped them become the person they are while inspiring and challenging others to do the same?*

That day, I was the one who had brought hope and help to others. For me, hope and help had always been a divinely appointed encounter that would save my life, redirect it, and put it on a more noble, sustainable path. What if I could catalyze those moments intentionally for the countless many who need to hear and know in their hearts that a better life is possible?

When I walked back into the house, I saw all around me the dissatisfaction of my house plans gone awry and knew there was a better way. The house and all its trappings had instantly become a defunct and misguided dream that were now liabilities in my true calling. I had found my purpose: to bring hope and help to people in need.

PART TWO

Making Purpose Reality

I walked into my office, sat down at my desk, which I call Hogtrails Central Command. (As a quick aside, here's how I got this name. I had started my consulting practice in 1984 under the name of Wittwer & Associates. In 1998, when my accountant told me that I should just plan to die broke on a beach, I decided to change the name to something that sounded more fun. Growing up in rural Kentucky, pigs were fixture of your daily life. They typically walk single file following what we called "pig trails," obedient little school children excelling in slop and mud. So, I changed the name permanently to Hogtrails, LLC, with the "hog" acting as a distant reference for Harley-Davidson motorcycles, which I love.) So, my desk, with its three twenty-one-inch monitor array and a nineteen-inch

LCD TV is always the place where the magic of deals, research, and creativity begins for me. I held my hands over my computer keyboard while staring at my blank screens. I had to catch this vision.

I felt like a composer about to craft a symphony or a painter seeing the finished work on his bare canvas. I glanced at the screens, their reminders of success like the virtuoso chairs of my string section. Taped above the monitor to the left is a fake $1,000,000 bill; the middle monitor a sign reading, "Sustainable Green," and above the right monitor a sign that reads, "Make the Call and It Will Be There." Hanging from the bottom of the TV to my far right, I nodded at four affirmations I had written down like the percussive backbone of what I was about to begin:

1) Focus on what is in front of you.

2) Get out of the house once a week.

3) Money will take care of itself.

4) Use your mind to work diligently only on things you can control.

I knew the power of Hogtrails Central Command, for I sat at that desk and made wildly lucrative calls. Now, I was contemplating something much greater than money or success— I was figuring out how to connect the past to the present in order to inspire the future. I lifted a nearby pen, and the first movement of my work was to determine my net worth, to see what I might contribute to make my idea reality. I calculated that if I liquidated everything, I could have upstart capital of $1,200,000. It was a breathtaking moment as I reflected that just over four years before I had $200 and a negative net worth of $35,000.

It was strange to cast my life in numbers, to see a figure that size staring back at me as an empty testimony to my new-found health and perspective. I asked myself, *How much am I willing to risk on a plan I don't have for people I will never meet?* I looked at the number again. It seemed so inanimate. I thought about all my wanderings in the motorhome and how the greatest joys came to me at the Waffle Houses and Walmarts whenever I could give something anonymously to help someone else or make a human connection.

Sharing the love gave me drive, desire, and purpose. After all, I had set up a revocable trust to benefit Give Kids the World in the event of my death. At that very moment, I thought about using my ability and capital to start something I could do in my lifetime and with my life. I sat there twirling the pen in my hand looking at my reminders and my net worth. *What does wealth win you except wealth?* I lectured myself.

I knew I was on the edge of a precipice, knew that when I jumped there was no turning back. I had reached a financial peak, especially in comparison to my past. I was afraid to throw it all away, to put it all up for grabs. But as I sat there, I knew that I could not *not* do this. At fifty-four, I still had time to fail and recover again as long as I had my health. However, I did not want to wake up at seventy, look back and say, "I wish I had done that!" It was like stumbling on an irreversible fact that can't be unlearned. And then I did it.

Without fanfare, just sitting at Hogtrails Central Command staring at my uncertain future in the face, I made the decision to *risk it all* for the chance to bring help and hope to others. Sitting in my empty house with the smell of old Ford trucks swirling around my head, with the rapt attention of young students and the tearful eyes of an appreciative teacher, I gave myself over to a larger purpose.

Have you ever resigned yourself to great risk with the potential for great reward? Asked the girl to marry you though you were scared? Started a business whose future was uncertain? Changed careers? The fear doesn't go away, but a sweet comfort floods your heart knowing that you at least dived in. With that comfort rolling over me in waves, I thought about my parents who said God had a plan for my life. For the first time since I'd had stepped foot on his green earth, I was sure I had found it.

The Middle Part Is Always the Longest

With the commitment question out of the way the next step was how. Once again I had to conjure the life of my hero, Colonel Harland Sanders, for inspiration and the stamina I knew this dream would require. When the Colonel sold Kentucky Fried Chicken in 1964, he kept the master franchise rights to Canada and Florida. He gave the rights to Florida to his daughter Margaret as a wedding present. In 1965, when he and his wife, Claudia, discovered that Canadian taxation was going to take half of the profits, well, the Colonel wouldn't stand for that. His solution would be no surprise if you knew the life story of Harland. He and Claudia established the non-profit Colonel Harland Sanders Charitable Foundation in which they placed all of the Canadian assets. A lifelong philanthropist even in the darkest days of his life and through multiple careers, the Colonel reasoned it was better to give the money made back to the people of Canada than their government. Each year when the profits were tallied, franchisees were asked where the money could best be spent in their communities. Most often it was to benefit children with hospital buildings or orphanages, the latter a real sweet spot for the Colonel.

I certainly didn't have the resources of the Colonel or the dependable revenue of a fast food franchise. But I do have grit and my firm belief in my theory of one degree—it had already demonstrated its power of connectivity and prosperity. Here is how things unfolded over the next three days while my head was spinning with ideas. First, I had to give the idea a name. People always smiled when I told them my business name was Hogtrails, so I started with that name and changed it a bit to HogStir. It sounded like fun, at least to me, and I was the only one in the plan so HogStir it would be for a little while. I was obviously reaching for straws at this point, but I didn't want to get caught by too much detail. I was more focused on the big picture. Then I started contemplating how I would use the trucks to gain awareness for the program and maybe engage the Ford Motor Company to help me.

How was I going to develop a group of people to get out and tell their stories? How was I going to build the extra capital? I had to put this in terms that would be fun for me and would resonate with others. I decided that I needed to develop a core group who believed in the idea as much as I did to tell their stories and who would be as tenacious trying to raise money. I had faith that, if given the opportunity to present my HogStir idea, people would want to help. There was no downside—I mean, how could people deny the opportunity to influence future generations by empowering them with hope? I needed to collect a "Gaggle of Geezers and Go-Getters" who would have stories to tell and in order to raise capital or services in kind I would create a national "Band of Beggars."

The next challenge was thinking about the delivery of the message in the schools. Not everyone who had a compelling story would be a good speaker or even have the ability to get in front of an audience. I began to think about how I could develop a DVD of my story and leave ten minutes at the end for presenters to add their own. This way, it would be a consistent approach to build confidence for presenters to where they eventually would not need the assistance.

The first three days of the HogStir program were sleepless for me. I was so excited about its potential. There were moments when I was so tired that all I could do was sit and stare, my mind sadly sputtering out strategies and tactics in its exhaustion. Still, I would not rest. My Dad's words just before his death would sneak into my plans, "I have all the money I need to do what I want but I don't have my health." I surveyed where I was to make sure I had taken a different road. I had all the money I needed to try and start this, and I had my health. I wasn't afraid. I believed in the power of one degree and had lived it. All I had to do was put myself out there and the connections would come. It was just like my mergers and acquisitions deals but this time I was brokering hope with a flat fee of inspiration and legacy.

During all this, I had been having trouble with the ignition and battery in my blue pickup, so I took it over to a parts store for a new battery. The alpine blue '51 was always a conversation starter wherever I parked. The parts store was certainly no exception. The attendant who helped me, a gentleman my age, came out to the truck.

As he changed my battery, I asked him if he knew anyone who may have a 1951 Ford panel truck. I had imagined that a panel truck would be a delivery vehicle for the message and that many in my generation would have fond memories of panel trucks delivering milk, eggs, and pastries to the doors of their childhood homes. He did not, but he suggested that I might want to attend the Turkey Day Hot Rod Run held every year in Daytona Beach. It sounded like a great idea to me. After all, on holidays I never had anywhere to go, so I got home and looked up the show and made my arrangements.

I spent Sunday looking through old car ads for a panel truck. None existed. I went over to my local 7-11 and, without even looking inside, I purchased a copy of *Truckin'* magazine. While checking out, I proclaimed to my friends behind the counter that one day I would have a 1951 Ford panel truck and it would be on the cover of the magazine. They were always kind and supportive but thought my boast was a little much and told me so. The manager was close to my age and he said he had not seen one of those in years. I took the magazine home and did not even open it.

On the afternoon of Thanksgiving Eve, I packed the Jeep and headed for Daytona and the Turkey Run. The number of hotrods and custom cars that were on the road made a parade of sound, color, and excitement. Complete strangers in gorgeous restorations were waving, revving their engines at each other, and having mock races on the highway down to Daytona. I arose early the next morning and made my way to the Speedway. I had a mission to find a panel truck. My mind and mission were like kelp in ocean drifts. As I walked in, I would just let my intuition guide me to the people and conversations that seemed right. Going through dozens of vehicles for a couple of hours, I spotted a 1952 Ford panel truck painted in black and pink.

I walked over and introduced myself to the couple who were the owners and asked if they wanted to sell the truck. They did not, but we chatted anyway, because that's what folks do at events like these. It's like stopping off at someone's front porch and letting them tell all about their hobby. You could just ask the question, "What's the story behind this one?" and folks could go on for hours. I completely understood. This couple talked about their truck and their love of the car culture. I talked about my HogStir idea along with challenges I had personally overcome.

As the conversation unfolded, it turned out that the lady had gastric bypass surgery several months before, was still losing weight, and her husband had paid for it with his retirement money so that she could have happiness while they were both alive. They had also adopted a son who had developed bipolar disorder and other challenges. If you were like me in those early days, you would think that this kind of commiseration was unusual, that finding people who personally knew the exact same challenges I did was just coincidence. But I found over time that these stories are *everywhere*. It showed me that the vision I had for creating moments of help and hope was for everyone, not just kids. The breadth of what I had envisioned grew larger still with conversations like these. When my chat with these new friends naturally came to a close, we shared some hugs and phone numbers. Then I left and I went about my search.

Theirs would be the only panel truck I saw that day. I was a little bummed, but it had still been a really cool day with all the cars and nice people. It wasn't a total waste as far as I was concerned. As I was leaving, though, I spotted a custom 1955 Ford pickup that was really special, but no one was around. I walked over to look at it and on the seat was a copy of *Mustang & Fords* magazine with the truck I was looking at on the cover. I wrote a note on my business card asking him to call me and dropped it on the seat next to the magazine.

Less than two hours later my phone rang and it was the owner of the pickup truck, John. I explained HogStir, and he told me that he wanted to meet me to talk about it. He had recently retired and sold an automotive parts business he had for thirty years. He also was a founding advisor for a technical program in Georgia, a college of sorts to learn the mechanics of motorsports. He had also been an accomplished professional racecar driver in his heyday. I told him I was headed home to Tampa, but he insisted that I get a room for the night and come back the next day to talk to him.

The next morning I got up early to head to the motorway because there was no guarantee John was going to be able to park his truck where it had been the day before. There were literally hundreds more hotrods and thousands more spectators. Every color you could imagine and some you cannot conceive covered the asphalt like a painter's panoply. Hoods were up everywhere exposing unnaturally large engines of gleaming metal and power. Flames adorned the sides of so many vehicles, some smoky blue from the end of a cigarette, some fiery red like fire from a dragon's mouth. The imagination of so many artisans had taken the mundane and made it explode like a metal parachute. I walked for two hours among the rows of cars so brilliant you thought they could only be constructed during a hallucinogenic trip. And then I saw John from afar standing next to his wheels. I called out his name over rumbling engines men had started just to hear the sound.

As I walked to his truck, out of the corner of my left eye, I spotted the familiar grille of a 1951 Ford truck. I looked over quickly, and I could hardly believe it—a 1951 Ford F-1 panel truck in a radiant baby blue was driving straight at me. I rushed over and asked the guy if he needed someplace to park. He said he had been circling for two hours trying to find a spot and was about to run out of gas. I pointed to the one vacant space in sight next to John, and he rolled in on fumes.

I walked over to the panel truck driver and asked if he wanted to sell it. He told me he had driven it from Chicago to sell it at the show, and he had the clear title in his pocket. I had been searching fiercely for a truck like this, and they started to seem more like a myth they were so rare. We quickly talked price. I was genuinely afraid that there was another panel truck maniac who would snatch up the gem before I could seal the deal.

Since John was right there and he was a true aficionado, I asked him to look it over and give me his assessment. According to John, it had good guts and lots of restoration potential though the interior needed plenty of work. I didn't wait a moment longer. I negotiated a price with the seller. We agreed he would take it back to Chicago where I would retrieve it, I walked to a bank to get a certified check for the initial deposit, and I bought the truck. I was perfectly euphoric. And to boot, after I regained my composure, John said he would be interested in helping HogStir.

It was Sunday afternoon after my purchase, I was back in Tampa, and I finally took the time to look through the *Truckin'* magazine I had from the 7-11.

I flipped to an article about the custom build of a 1941 Willys pickup truck that had competed for national awards. It had been restored and modified by Legens Hot Rod in Martin, Tennessee, and the article had a picture of the business owner and his crew. I looked at a road atlas and made a plan to pass through Martin on my way from Chicago.

I emailed the owner and gave him the elevator pitch about my plan. Along with it I sent a picture of the panel truck I had purchased and described its needs. I had a response from him first thing the next morning. It simply read, "I want to help. Please call me."

I picked up the phone immediately and dialed. When I got the owner, Steve Legens, on the phone, I asked why my email sparked his interest. Outside of the needs of my panel truck, he and his wife have three sons, and as parents, they knew the challenges of parenthood and inspiration. He also shared with me that they are very active in their church and that he himself could have been considered an "at risk" youth. Just from my brief description, he believed in the concept of my plan and wanted to be a part of it. I told him I would drive the panel truck through Martin and we could talk about the program and the truck.

That same day, on my way into Tampa, I drove along an unfamiliar highway taking me to a part of downtown where I didn't usually travel. I spotted what appeared to be the rear end of a 1951 or '52 Ford truck stopped in the emergency lane. I slowed down and saw he had the hood up and definitely had problems. I was no stranger to that condition with my own trucks. I pulled over and as I began to back up to help, I could see the man walk toward my Jeep.

I rolled the window down and asked if I could help. He said he had recently put a new engine in the truck, it had failed, and he already had help on the way. I told him that I had two 1951 Ford F-1 pickups at home and from the passenger seat pulled up a picture of the panel truck I had just purchased. His eyes glowed with excitement as he told me he had been rebuilding 1951 Ford trucks for more than twenty years.

In an instant, he held up his business card, and on the card it had a picture three different sizes and series of 1951 Ford trucks. He said he had just sold his '51 panel truck and if I was interested, I should come over to his house to see his 1951 Ford fire truck. I took his card, and with assurance that he was getting the help he needed, I drove off.

I called my roadside friend a couple of days later and went to see the fire truck. As I approached the beast sitting lifeless in the yard, most people would have seen an old rusty heap with a lot of work to be done. I did not. I saw a restored, bright red fire truck with a bunch of kids hanging off of it in a parade with my program logo on the side. The chrome grille on the front was gleaming with the spring sun and the sheen on the perfect paint job shimmered. Just imagine a group of elementary school students sitting in history class when this puppy pulled up to their parking lot. I could see their excitement in my mind's eye, see their hearts opening up to the message of hope HogStir would give them.

My imagination gave way to reality standing in front of the fire truck, the custom paint job melted away to show rust once again and the gleaming chrome oxidized back to its current painted state. Call me crazy. I had nowhere to put it, no way to work on it, but I bought it anyway. I was following the divine drift of having met this man on the roadside, and there was a warm, intuitive assurance that this was the right thing to do.

After buying the truck, I learned that the 1951 model year Ford fire truck was one of the most replicated die-cast models and that many volunteer fire departments across the country had owned this model and year of truck. I imagined the fully restored fire truck towering over the 1/100 scale model next to it, a gift we would give the children at our presentations and possibly even sell to establish a revenue stream.

The following week, I flew to Chicago to retrieve my panel truck. It had been snowing, and I was about to drive an old truck with a 350 Chevy hot rod engine twelve hundred miles to Tampa. Even worse, the truck was full of loose, old parts that reminded me of their presence at the slightest bump. Imagine riding inside of a snare drum with someone beating on it for hours! The heater was more of a warmer at best, and with my acclimation to Florida's climate, the Illinois land-scape might as well have been the Siberian steppe.

Driving from Chicago, shivering in the cold with no radio, I had a lot of time to think. I surveyed over and over where I had come so far and where I needed to go to keep my plan moving. I came up with an idea to create a "Possibilities Group" with some of my neighbors. There were so many successful businesspeople within a stone's throw, I knew I could learn from their experiences and get their insights about my plan. I decided to invite seven men to my home who were each in different industries, with the caveat that each of them had to own or manage a large international, national, or regional business.

None of the seven would be in the same industry or work in a business together. This would keep the interests diverse. I also thought it might be a good icebreaker for each of them to develop a sense of community within our small group of homes. I sent seven invitations and all RSVP'd that they were interested and would attend. Now, I hoped to have a core group of bright minds to assist in developing a plan.

Where the Rubber Meets the Road

I was fortunate to acquire a new mergers and acquisitions client in early December that is publicly traded on the NASDAQ. I was retained under exclusive contract to acquire massage therapy schools across the United States. We identified twenty prospective acquisitions from California to Connecticut, and I had six months to make things happen. The moment the gate of opportunity opens for me, I sit down at Hogtrails Central Command, look at the fake million-dollar bill, and start dialing for dollars. In two days, I had all twenty prospects on the phone and several appointments on the books.

Acquisitions work is typically about long lead times, planting seeds, staying top-of-mind with a potential acquisition, and finding the middle ground for the people involved, the place where the price feels right to everyone. I try not to wear out my welcome or push too hard at the beginning. Folks have to make up their own minds. And usually there's enough money at stake that one guy trying to convince them one way or another is futile. Also, it's usually someone's life work—their small business that boomed, their parents' business they inherited—that you're offering to buy. It's no small thing for them, so I just step back while they go through their process, and when the match and timing is right, well, I make sure I'm at the right place at the right time.

My first stops for this new client were in California, and because I was close to Arizona, I decided to spend the holiday in Prescott and truly get a sense of whether it could be my next home. Despite the party with Maria and the new group of accomplished men that would be assembling at my house, I had to be ever mindful of my illnesses. Good relationships and success would be instantly undone if my challenges came home to roost again. Moving away from the hurricanes was still a top priority. There are some storms from which you can only run away.

From Prescott, I was flying to Connecticut to get back on my acquisitions schedule. As I boarded the plane, the Southwest flight in Las Vegas, I scanned for a seat next to a person that might have a good story to tell. On this particular flight, seat 2D had headphones on—no good. Seat 5C—sleeping. But a few rows back, I definitely saw a good story sitting in an aisle seat. It was an older fellow, possibly in his seventies, wearing an NFL Fox Sports ball cap and a brown leather flight jacket. His grizzled face and kind eyes spoke of a man who had both loved and lost, who had known victory and defeat, power and helplessness. Yes, there was definitely a story there. I quickly jumped to the window seat and waited for the plane to get high above the earth to start a conversation. I could sense that there was a one-degree connection to be made. Whether it would lead to anywhere for my mission, I wasn't too concerned about that at this point. You can never know where things will lead.

The obvious connecting point for average man-to-man talk would have been the ball cap. But I thought the greater story was probably in the jacket and all that it had seen, so I started talking about when I learned to fly in my twenties. Soon he told me he was a pilot and about how he'd joined the Air Force where he had a twenty-plus-year career. He talked of flying in Vietnam and all the other renowned military hot spots in the world he had seen with a perfect aerial view.

Our conversation progressed and we got more comfortable with each other. We introduced ourselves—we'll call this fellow Mr. X—and I finally asked about the ball cap.

"I work for the company," he replied.

"You don't look like you play football," I said.

"No, I work for Fox. I am in charge of flight operations for the company and have been Rupert Murdoch's personal pilot for twenty-one years. Now, I have two pilots who answer to me, but I still fly the boss on some of the long runs." And there I was, one degree from Rupert Murdoch, a global media giant. I didn't pry too much. You have to be sensitive to people who are close to power. Too many people try to work agendas through a powerful man's entourage. If I ever wanted to have true help from this man and the world he was connected to, I would have to be nonchalant about it. After a couple of hours of general conversation, I briefly told Mr. X about my plan and prefaced it with, "When I tell you about this, I am not trying to find a way to the boss." He politely listened as the plane started its landing sequence. I could tell he was walking through the flight procedures in his mind as I talked.

We rolled into the gate, deplaned, and when we reached the terminal, I gave him my card. Truthfully, I never expected to see him again, but hearing his story and connecting with him was enough for now.

The next day, I went to meet the owner of the massage school I had targeted. I was there to convince him to sell his school to my client. You can tell so much from people in a few moments of a first meeting. The owner, Steve Kitts, was soft-spoken and wore run-of-the-mill jeans. I could tell instantly he was a genuine soul. We took a tour of the Connecticut Center for Massage Therapy (CCMT) Newington campus and talked for an hour about the school business and how his company could fit with my client's well-established operation.

And then conversation swept us up. After the business talk had run its course, we took the next three hours sharing about our own lives, principles of benevolence and faith, and how he and his wife have incorporated the well-being of the *whole* person into their school's curriculum, including touch therapy for children with emotional illnesses. I'm sure it's no surprise to you that I talked about my idea. Steve and I had a lot in common when it came to helping and healing people whose physical and emotional challenges would jeopardize their quality of life.

I spoke of the energy, resolve, and imagination it would take to establish and sustain my idea. He interjected that I was overlooking one key component of making the program successful: surrender. I asked what he meant by that, and he explained that I had to surrender my complete being to its success. Whatever it took, I must do.

With the day wrapping to a close, it was obvious that our time together had come to an end. I left with a good feeling about Steve and his company, and we would continue the acquisition dance through email and phone calls.

On the morning of December 30, I headed back to the airport, dropped off my rental car, and hastily got on the shuttle bus. As I hopped on, there was only one other passenger in the rear. And wouldn't you know it, it was Mr. X. What are the odds? We spent two hours together before we had to go our separate ways. He said he had been thinking about that "program" of mine, and if I ever made it materialize, he may talk to the boss for me. "But don't count on it," he smirked, "I don't normally get involved."

I took him at his word because he was definitely a what-you-see-is-what-you-get sort of guy. And whether he ever would help me, I'm okay with not knowing. My idea was just like my business: you plant seeds, let people make their own choices, and any affinity they have for your success is because of their own choosing. I have Mr. X's contact information ready and waiting.

7

Surrender to Purpose

The New Year of 2007 rang in at my house while I was in a sleep closer to a coma. I had worn myself out over the past three weeks crisscrossing the country for my idea and my business. But as tiring as it was, it was also immensely exciting. It was a big idea with inscrutable gaps around those aspects where I had little or no knowledge. I didn't know anything about curriculum, publishing, rules and regulations for people entering school grounds, web development and media venues, and the list went on and on.

In the first few days of January, as happened many times in those early days, I wrestled with conflicted feelings of giving up before I really started. Another troubling thing was that every time I talked about the program to anyone, it made me weepy. Reliving my story over and over was painful—I couldn't turn off the waterworks when I thought about changing the lives of others. Every time I spoke about my challenges, it was like the sixth grade faces were peering up at me full of unblemished possibility.

And whenever I would think of those children, I thought about family trees and the exponential hope and healing that could shake the very foundations of our world. What if just ten, one hundred, one thousand people could chart a new, healthful course for their lives? The endless possibility of love and hope shook me to my core. I knew I couldn't let go of the idea. I was going to stick to it to my last dime, whatever it took. My personal faith in God and his plan for my life told my heart what I had to do. I had to surrender *all*.

I used to sing the hymn "I Surrender All" growing up in church. I pulled out the *Broadman Hymnal* from a piano bench in my house. I opened its faded cover and flipped the wafer-thin pages. I found that familiar song, one that influenced the generations who had sung it. I read through the lines and watched the musical notes dance and the clefs throb. I let the song come alive in me, and I found the solace I needed in its verses and refrain to continue on into the unknown.

The first meeting of my new Possibilities Group was scheduled for the evening of January 11. I was going to make it a really special evening so the participants would be inspired to make this a regular monthly get-together. I had a chef come to the house to cook, and I had purchased a sixty-inch round table that comfortably seated eight so that all could see everyone around the table.

On the afternoon of our gathering, I got out my four trucks, including the fire truck, and placed them in the driveway for the guys to see. It looked like a 1951 Ford dealership.

The guys trickled in one by one, and our evening began. I welcomed everyone and thanked them for coming. I explained that the Possibilities Group was designed for face-to-face gatherings where we could field ideas collectively. Sure, I wanted to talk about my idea, but I also wanted to hear these successful and inspiring men talk about their businesses and business challenges.

After my quick introduction, I asked each of them to share who they were and their type of business with the others. The table consisted of people who were high school dropouts to those who had multiple graduate degrees. All of them were successful business people. It became quick to see that your latitude is determined by your attitude! Two had most unusual stories of their upbringing and success.

One was raised on the streets of London. His parents were street merchants who sat up shop each day on different street corners around the city. His mother had hand sewn different pockets in her dresses to hide money, so when she got robbed, a thief wouldn't get all of the day's earnings. During his upbringing, this guy had become quite the brawler and found himself in street bouts all the time. But his parents were determined to change their situation, if not for themselves then for their children. He and his brother got good educations, and he eventually became an attorney and moved to the states working for British Petroleum as a "solicitor," British for attorney. Once here, he discovered the timeshare resort industry and had spent his career doing that instead of law. And though it's random, it's too fantastic not to mention that he was also the first bass player for Atom and the Antz (and his math teacher in high school, Brian May, became the lead guitarist for the music group Queen).

Another guest had an even more captivating story. He grew

up malnourished in an alcoholic family in Chicago and quit school at age seventeen. He joined the Marines with some friends under the Buddy program. In order to enlist, you had to weigh at least 115 pounds and at five feet seven inches Andy Gerovac weighed 113. The recruiters took him across the street to McDonald's and started feeding him hamburgers until he couldn't eat any more. They took him back and weighed him and he was still light, so they put the remaining hamburgers in his hands to get him above 115. In the Marines, he had muscled up to a whopping 125 pounds when they shipped him out to Vietnam as a machine gunner where every day he had to carry his weight in food, gear, guns, and ammunition through the jungle.

After the Vietnam War, Andy returned to Chicago to find that his parents had thrown out all of his possessions and had essentially disowned him. He eventually went to Buffalo, New York, where he had a friend who also was a machine gunner and together they had shared six months in foxholes in Vietnam. Andy talked about his experience of being homeless in Buffalo after the war living in his car and bathing under a cup of water in public restrooms and drying off with paper towels. He finally got a job at a body shop, and every night he and one of his friends would try to think of a business they could start. Finally, they decided on Mexican restaurants because there were virtually none in Buffalo. At the time of our Possibilities Group, The Mighty Taco, the venture by a once-homeless Vietnam Veteran, had grown to sixteen locations and hundreds of employees.

The next morning, I got emails from several of those who

came. And Mighty Taco man said he wanted to host the group in his home in February. The idea for the Possibilities Group had some traction.

Sam

I had a school visit the next day with another acquisition prospect in Texas. It went well, but was not the spark I expected. There's a multiplicity of key identifiers of the right or wrong deal and business seller. I have no formal training in accounting, law, or any of the normal professional skills in my profession. I just have the School of Hard Knocks diploma and the experience of working in a variety of industries over the course of twenty-five years. It doesn't take long to size up a potential deal or evaluate the prospective seller's intent. You must have firsthand knowledge and see both the seller and the business to best determine whether it's viable. Because the school I visited didn't seem like a good target, I decided to catch a late evening flight home to Tampa rather than stay on and continue my investigation.

I boarded the plane and in the fifth row window seat there was an interesting looking guy. He was gazing out mindlessly, and as I made my way down the aisle, he turned to look at me. He had long, oily hair to his shoulders, tattered clothes, and I could tell without him opening his mouth that at least four or more front teeth were missing. I had spotted a story for the ride back to Tampa, and I sat in the aisle seat. He looked surprised that anyone would choose to sit next to him.

When the plane reached cruise altitude, I leaned over and introduced myself. He said his name was Sam. Almost instantly, he came to life and began talking. He spent a good deal of time recalling his mother, who had died the year before. I asked why he was going to Tampa, and he said he lived there. I sensed he was homeless as his evasive answer to "Where in Tampa do you live?" revealed. Politely, I told him I had had a few challenges in my life, including homelessness. I could see it in his eyes, I had hit the raw nerve, and he told me he was indeed homeless. I stepped around the topic for a few minutes and then asked him how he happened to be on the plane that night coming from Houston.

Sam was flown to Houston by NASA to be evaluated for an extended sleep study. NASA had advertised to find participants for the study. For a homeless guy, it was a good gig, for the most part. They would pay travel, three months of hotel, and per diem for applicants. The one downside—and there's always a downside to such studies—is that the participant had to remain on a bed slanted at six degrees, awake or asleep for a period of three months straight in a laboratory environment. They wanted to understand the effects of extended sleep on potential flights to other planets.

If Sam were selected, he would be paid a fairly handsome sum, $17,200, and he planned to use the money to have his teeth done in Mexico. Unfortunately, he had an abscessed tooth and a urinary tract infection, and NASA had given him a ticket to Tampa and instructions to go to a clinic for treatment before he could join the study. I asked why they sent him to Tampa, if he was homeless. NASA had decided to send him there for warmer weather. On the night our plane would land, it would be forty-six degrees in Tampa. His clothes and coat where in shambles.

This was a perfect opportunity to share some love. But I was unsure how to do it without his knowledge or embarrassing him. I decided to go to the rear of the plane and talk to the Southwest flight attendants, one man and two women, to enlist their help. I ingratiated myself to them by sharing some highlights of my longstanding Rapid Rewards customer relationship with Southwest. I also told them a bit about my life experiences of overcoming mental illness, homelessness, and obesity—my perfect segue.

"I'm telling you all this," I said, "because it just so happens that one of your passengers, the guy I'm sitting next to, is homeless, penniless, and flying into forty-six degree weather in Tampa."

The attendants looked at me a little stunned. I'm sure this was different from their standard interaction with passengers. As I told them about Sam, I pulled out my wallet.

"Tonight," I said, "we are going to share some l-o-v-e, not l-u-v, the stock ticker symbol for Southwest." I pulled all of the money out of my wallet, close to two hundred dollars, and asked them if they would please put it in an envelope along with bags of peanuts and snack boxes and give it to my fellow passenger just before the plane landed.

"If you want to toss in a few dollars, great. If not, that's fine," I said as I handed them the money. "There are only a couple of conditions. Please tell him that Southwest wants to share some love. And please don't tell him it was me." There were some quick agreements and wordless head shakes. Then I returned to my seat. In all, it took about five minutes. I hoped it seemed like a bathroom trip to Sam.

The captain came on the overhead announcing the landing sequence, and an attendant came forward and handed Sam a sizable black bag of goodies along with a sealed envelope. They insisted he *not* open the envelope until we landed and that Southwest wanted to share some love. He was genuinely surprised and wanted to open the envelope, but I stopped him.

Within minutes we touched down, taxied to the gate, and deplaned. I decided to wait with Sam to get off the plane. As others passed us, he pulled out a tiny bag from overhead and slipped on a ragged jacket with its pockets ripped open. They seemed like tears from others trying to rob him. He walked ahead of me, and I was the last to deplane. The flight attendants were there to see us off, and we all passed warm, knowing glances at each other with our misty eyes. Just before I left, one of the female attendants pounced at me with a kiss on the cheek and whispered a warm "Thank you" in my ear.

Sam and I walked into the concourse. I asked him where he was going, but he had no clue. I asked how he planned to get there, and again he had no idea. I so wanted to help him but knew that sometimes you're only meant to help for a little while or in a small way. As we walked a little further, Sam peeled off and made his way to a gate full of empty seats. I continued to walk on and caught him out of the corner of my eye as he sat down and fished through the bag. As I rounded a corner, the last thing I saw was Sam holding the envelope.

More Possibilities

Working in mergers and acquisitions is nerve racking, stressful, and exhilarating all at the same time. You have to think of it as a game. You can't think about what a million dollars means. You certainly can't count on a predictable income, unless you have had years of filling a pipeline with deals and prospects. You have to pick your assignments very carefully. If your client does not have a history of closing deals, they are a waste of time. If they do not have a good story to tell, they are a waste of time. If the potential number of prospective companies to acquire is too small, it is a waste of time.

The company with whom I contracted to acquire massage therapy schools, Steiner Leisure LTD, was (and is) a great organization with a great story to tell. But there were too few target companies, and they were almost all small—much smaller than I had anticipated. I had also signed an agreement that limited my ability to work for any other school company during my assignment, which would ultimately kill my prospect pipeline at a critical time. It was becoming more and more apparent the assignment may not yield much, and I had four months to go to meet my six-month acquisitions deadline.

Along with my work, I had continued my obsession about my program. I called all over the place looking for trucks and parts. I browsed the Internet looking at all kinds of websites and business models. I began to research development of a nonprofit organization and capital partners to help me in the initial launch. A busy, busy bee was I.

In February, the second meeting of the Possibilities Group was going to be held at Andy's house complete with food from his own Mighty Taco recipes. I sent an invitation out to the people who had attended the meeting at my house informing them that I wanted to present my concept for a nonprofit business.

They gave me ten minutes to present my idea. I cast the vision for inspiring children and enabling hurting people of all ages to face their challenges and overcome them. I talked about my plan to develop awareness with the unique use of antique cars and a fire truck that I would restore and had been calling the Funkee Fire truck. And as I wrapped up my presentation, Dave the Englishman jumped in with a crucial question. "Paul, who is your customer?"

I was caught flat-footed. I had never thought of the program having a customer. But it made sense. If my dream was going to sustain itself, it would need a customer of sorts, a way to create an influx of operating capital that was consistent with the mission of the organization. I told the group, stumbling through an answer, that I had imagined making a die-cast model of my panel truck to sell for a revenue stream. But he wasn't asking about revenue at all, his question was, "Who needs this inspiration?"

One of the group members continued, "Okay, so, you go

in and tell a story. You get kids and adults pumped up to take action, and then what? What are you going to do to give them some way to realize their inspiration?" If I was flat-footed before, now I completely face-planted. What *was* I going to do? It was so obvious that I can't believe I hadn't thought of it before. You give someone hope and then you have to give them help.

Another group member jumped in, the father of the two girls who originally sent me on this great mission with their request to the Teach-In. "Paul, David's right. You've got to understand the customer. And I think your strategy of using the fire truck could be brilliant. But, your idea could be much bigger than you have imagined, something that could entice the Ford Motor Company." This gentleman worked for the financing arm of Ford located in Nashville, so he knew some of the ins and outs. I tucked that away and tried not to get too excited or expectant. I have a natural tendency to run through possibilities quickly in my mind, and I can envision in the space of ten seconds something that could take months or years to actually accomplish. Still, this Ford connection could be the real deal, and the next day I received the names and contact information for the right people at Ford who might help. The irony was, it was *his* wife and daughters who had started me on this journey in the first place, selling at my door.

As other members discussed their businesses, I was still firing ideas through my mind about HogStir. I was listening and not listening. I was latching onto any possible tidbit from their worlds that could possibly help mine. As the guys continued to talk, they discovered that they all played guitars and were avid music lovers. The Mighty Taco host had us watch a DVD of the Las Vegas Blue Man Group for a few minutes. During the Blue Man video, they had a guy who came onstage playing a musical instrument that wrapped around him like an octopus and was worn like a big backpack. While playing and walking, the instrument began to shoot streamers and confetti across the crowd.

I looked at Andy and said, "There it is! That is what I need to shoot T-shirts out of the Funkee Fire Truck!" From that night onward, the Possibilities Group would taper down. We wouldn't continue it much longer as a formal group, though several guys would remain part of my journey. The momentum of my life was gaining speed, and the group had fulfilled its purpose and then some. I had so many things to pursue, which required me to strike out to try and make a difference.

Phone Call After Phone Call

The next day, I got on the phone and called the offices of the Blue Man Group in Las Vegas to find out where I could get one of those contraptions I saw on the DVD. They told me it was a proprietary technology developed specifically for their performances, and I would need to call a company called Artistry in Motion if I wanted to know more. When I called, they asked who had referred me to them. I said the Blue Man

Group in Las Vegas, and I was put straight to the owner of the company, Richard Graves.

I explained my program idea and the concept of the Funkee Fire Truck for televised parades. "So you are calling me because you need help with its funkification," Richard interjected. "Yes," I said, "from the looks of your website and products it appears you have a lot of experience with funkification." He said he liked my program idea and that he would give it some thought and would email me with ideas.

It is one thing to have a big idea, but you really have to be sure that the crazy thing you believe in is even plausible much less possible. Before I went too far out on a limb, I needed to find the experts who knew parades. Once again I turned to my "Super Sniffer" and the power of Hogtrails Central Command to find the answers on a Friday afternoon. I Googled a lot of terms until I found the correct combination, "Events and Festivals," and there it was, the International Festivals and Events Association (IFEA) located in, of all places, Boise, Idaho. I quickly perused their website and picked up the phone to place a call to Steve Schmader, president and CEO of the organization. In keeping with my usual good fortune, he was in and answered his phone.

I introduced myself and explained the reason for my call, the Funkee Fire Truck, and my vision for my program. Let me put this in a bit of perspective. The IFEA Mission clearly stated on their website, "To inspire and enable those in our industry to realize their dreams, build community, and sustain success through celebration." And on the other end of the phone is Mr. Schmader who has graciously taken the call—I am cranked up about a junky fire truck and a big idea. What better person to talk to than him? Oh yeah, the guy I had on the phone literally helps people celebrate all over the world *every day*!

Steve liked my idea so much he said, "Paul I am going to give you the name and number of the one person who can put you on the right track for televised parades, and in particular, the Macy's Day Parade. You need to call Ms. Jean McFaddin and here is her number."

"Who is Ms. McFaddin?" I asked.

"Jean ran the Macy's Day parade for twenty-five years and built it into the colossus it has become. She also has been instrumental in authoring the operation and safety guidelines for parades around the world. She is retired now but still does some consulting. I think she would like to hear your story and can point you in the right direction. Please keep me posted. I like your vision and that Funkee Fire Truck could be fun!"

And there I was, on a late Friday afternoon, within one degree of Jean McFaddin who had helped hundreds of millions of us wake up each Thanksgiving morning to the spectacle of the Macy's Day Parade. I got on the Internet after the call to research "Jean McFaddin" and oh what a wonderful career she has had!

The following Monday I placed a call to the number Steve Schmader had given me, but I only got a recording. I was a bit let down, but I leave a good voice mail that inspires return calls. After all, I am known as the "Pleasant Pest." A few days later my cell phone rang and I could see the area code was New York City. My heart pounded in my chest with hope and anticipation. *Could it be Ms. McFaddin?* Indeed it was!

She introduced herself and spryly said, "How can I help you?"

I am not one to get shaky on the phone, but in that instant my mind went a little blank as visions of giant balloons, marching bands, kids on parents' shoulders, and me as a kid lying on the floor Thanksgiving Day watching the parade raced through my head.

I brought my composure into focus and slowly began to talk about my vision for the program I wanted to develop, the Funkee Fire Truck, and my affinity for old Ford trucks. I don't know why I brought up the latter, it just came out.

"I am a Ford person too," she said. "I just sold my 1964 ½ Ford Mustang that I bought new. My family has always been a Ford family because my father spent his whole career with Ford Motor Credit."

We spent a few moments connecting about Ford, and she jumped to it, asking what help she could offer. I explained my needs for direction, if a vehicle like I was proposing could even be in the parades, under what category, safety requirements, etc. She graciously answered all of my questions and gave me direction to other resources. She said she would like to help but had retired due to severe health challenges. She did, however, invite me to email the progress and if she felt she could, she may help me. Not a promise, just a maybe. I ended the call with a "Thank You" that probably sounded like a ten-year-old that had just seen Santa in the Thanksgiving Day Parade. My conversation with Ms. McFaddin was indeed all of that to me. Balloons and old fire trucks danced in my head.

———

I knew after the second Possibilities Group that I was going to have to make a move from Florida to see the program realized. I couldn't handle another season of hurricane stress and remain sold-out to the vision of helping others. I had purchased a home building site in Prescott, Arizona, the month before without selling either of my homes in Tampa. It was a real stretch, but at the time I had a lot of equity in my Florida homes. But then the market had started turning sour, and it would get worse in the soon-to-come 2008 year. I was only eight weeks into my budding vision, and I realized I had made a big mistake in buying property in Prescott. With the vision taking shape in my mind—and with my life direction having drastically changed since my life's purpose flooded into my life—I knew Prescott wasn't the right location. It wasn't close enough to media and opportunities. But I didn't want to live in Los Angeles or New York either . . . too metropolitan. It dawned on me then, what about Nashville? It was, I had come to understand, a sort of "third coast" with plenty of media and entertainment. Plus, I sensed it would be more ripe for capital and talent to help me with my vision.

Despite the melee I was in with all my real estate, I made a decision on faith to move to Nashville. It was blind faith.

I had lived in Walmart parking lots and Kamp Grounds of

America (KOA) for several months while working on the Nashville Auto Diesel College acquisition in 2002. I had grown to think of Nashville as the epicenter of hope with its hundreds of churches along with its Christian and country music industries. The people are friendly and most of them have an accent with a Southern drawl like mine. In Nashville, when you first meet someone, they don't ask what you do. No, they ask where you are from and where you go to church. If you are not going to church, they invite you to theirs. I also wanted to be in Nashville because I believed when HogStir got legs I would need to travel, and Southwest has plenty of flights out of the Nashville International airport. Within less than two hours, I could reach 60 percent of the U.S. population.

I mulled over the program development, worked my mergers and acquisitions business, and planned a move. I was still consumed by the idea for the Funkee Fire Truck. On a Sunday afternoon, I was watching a one-hour documentary about Walt Disney Imagineering located in Glendale, California. During the program, they kept interviewing Larry Gertz, a twenty-year creative vice president of the Imagineering group. I thought he would be the perfect person to contact to help me with my fire truck and program. I figured he had to live close to Glendale, so I found a residential number that might be him in Pasadena. I called and left a message about my needs and idea.

A couple of days later, I was watching a television program that featured a celebrity hot rod run sponsored by *Hot Rod* magazine. Some of the people featured I had heard of, but one I had not, Larry Wood. He was introduced as the Chief

Designer and one of the originators of Mattel Hot Wheels. That had my instincts engaged! I listened intently and thought about how someone like Larry could really help me design the Funkee Fire Truck and maybe get me in the door at Mattel. I decided to call Larry Wood too.

I looked up the number for Mattel corporate headquarters in El Segundo, California and dialed. The automated attendant told me to punch in the name of the party to whom I wanted to speak. I spelled out Larry Wood, it rang, and he picked up the phone, "Larry Wood." I was a little stunned it was that easy. I introduced myself, and told him the reason for my call and what I thought I might be able to do with the Funkee Fire Truck. I shared with him that I had spoken with Artistry in Motion and had a call into a Disney Imagineer. He liked the idea, especially the "funkification" of the fire truck. He gave me his email, asked me to send him more on my idea. He said he would be in touch, and if I was ever in the area I was welcome to visit. All of that from one call after watching a TV show.

That evening I went over to Target and stood in the die-cast toy aisle. Moms and children were crowding in negotiating what they could or could not have. I had a Hot Wheels model in my hands. I turned it over and over, inspecting all the details, imagining what a fire truck might look like at this small scale. I wondered if it could truly generate income for the program. I left Target sensing I had a decent idea. Granted, my fire truck wouldn't be the new iPod, but from that one piece of market research, I thought there could possibly be some legitimacy to the direction.

Two days later, I received a call on my cell from a number I did not recognize. "Hello," I answered. "Mr. Wittwer, this is Larry Gertz, you had called last Sunday and I am just now getting back to you because I had problems with my voice mail. How can I help you?"

I explained my program idea and the concept I had for the Funkee Fire Truck. He told me that he had retired from Disney and before he became an Imagineer, he was a college professor, so he understood the value of my program idea. Larry asked for my contact information and said he would like to be involved and would send me follow-up ideas and a proposal. He told me he was working on the development of a World War II aircraft museum in Seattle for Paul Allen, the cofounder of Microsoft. And there I was again, a few calls brought the help of an Imagineer and placed me one degree from Paul Allen.

Music City

Things were moving fast in all departments. I was planting seeds for the program and trying to find a plot of ground to plant my own roots. I decided to fly down and meet with a Nashville realtor. We drove all around the south of town, and of all that we saw, I had a conflicted interest in one of the properties—a 1950s ranch sitting on three acres on Franklin Pike in a nice area called Oak Hill.

The reason I say *conflicted* is because the house was just a notch above squalor inside and out. The yard was overtaken with brush and trees that had gone unchallenged for years, decades even. The inside could make you faint. It had a curious and unsavory smell and the aura of leftover chaos and overcrowding. It looked like a recently vacated packrat heaven.

The one thing the property had in its favor was location. At the first visit, the realtor pointed to several nearby mansions and said things like, "governor of Tennessee" and "Martina McBride" and "Ronnie Milsap." I did a little research of my own and learned the CEO of Gaylord Entertainment (of Grand Ole Opry and Opryland Hotel fame) also lived there, directly across the street. Despite the home's immense challenges—it had been advertised as a "tear down"—I asked myself one simple question, "Do I believe that I can buy the property and develop relationships with the people in the neighborhood to help with my program?" My unsold properties in Florida and Arizona were snickering, and I sensed that perhaps this wasn't the wisest financial move. But that was overridden by the possibility of having influential advocates for my program.

As I stood there in my thoughts, a tour bus pulled up to the stop sign near the house. I could see the driver talking on a microphone. This had to be a special place for the tour buses to roll through.

I decided I would do it. I called the realtor in Nashville and told her I was coming back up to look at the house again. As I mentioned, I was compelled to surrender all. And in this instance, "surrender" meant making a fairly unwise financial decision. I didn't care if it would take me closer to fulfilling my purpose. With a few phone calls to my other realtors, I power-priced my other properties to get them out of the picture. I called my banker with my plans for a move to Nashville and got his assent and promise for help.

In a few short days, we negotiated a deal, and I returned the following weekend to begin the process to claim my new "prize." As I walked through it again and arranged home inspections and all that, I really began to question myself, but I still believed in where I was going and what I wanted to do.

The following day, I signed up for one of the area bus tours called "Homes of the Stars." The tour started at Gaylord Opryland Hotel, then drove by Grand Ole Opry and on to Music Row. We then began to drive out Franklin Pike. Soon we were in Oak Hill and just as the bus passed my property it slowed to show the home of John and Martina McBride, then turned down what the driver called "Millionaires' Row." We passed the Governor's Mansion, the former home of Minnie Pearl and other greats, then stopped at the sign on Franklin Pike so the driver could talk about the homes of Ronnie Milsap on the left and Colin Reed, CEO of Gaylord Entertainment, on the right. Mr. Reed's home was built by country legend Webb Pierce whose biggest hit, "There Stands the Glass," is regarded as one of country's classic drinking songs. The home is known for its large guitar-shaped swimming pool in the back. Directly out the front window of the bus was my future home.

The tour wound its way around until we took a pit stop two hours in. I walked up to the bus driver, introduced myself, and asked him if he remembered the old ranch-style house for sale during the tour. He did, and I told him I had just bought it. He looked at me with surprise and said, "Do you know where you are going to be living?" "Yes," I said, "I just took the tour." We all boarded the bus again, and started back up Franklin Pike north to return to where we started. I was sitting on the back row when we pulled up to a traffic light a half mile from my new home. The driver looked in the rear view mirror and asked, "Paul, is it all right if I show people your new home off Millionaires' Row?" The bus got silent as if I might be somebody! "Sure," I replied.

As we slowed down in front of Martina's home, the driver grabbed his microphone. "Ladies and gentlemen, you remember Martina's home here on the left and next to her is Colin Reed. If you look to your right you see the new home of Paul Wittwer sitting on the back row." I had a contract on the house for one day and it was already on the tour. I asked everyone to overlook its appearance and to come back in two years. A few months later, I was working in the yard and heard a horn honking. I looked to the street and there sat a little tour bus driven by the same driver. He had everyone on the bus waving at me.

———

Through my efforts to figure out the best business model for HogStir, I first thought of starting as a nonprofit, which would require begging for funds or using my own money. But I discovered the Center for NonProfit Management based in Nashville and shared my idea with them. They explained the concept of a for-profit, for-benefit model with a tandem 501c3 nonprofit. They gave me the example of Paul Newman's brand, Newman's Own (the guy whose face you see on salad dressings).

Well, that sure sounded like a better idea and probably a more compelling way to engage people and sponsors in the effort. When you're trying to start something, there's a subtle respectability to engineering it to sustain itself. Its attraction is through its success rather than its call for sympathy and donations. I also liked the idea of building a self-sustaining business that could carry on without me. Despite my health accomplishments, I still had the nagging feeling that my days were numbered regardless of my progress.

———

Ever since one of the Possibility Group members had given me connections to Ford, I had been building up to the moment I would approach them. The time had come in March 2007. I sent an email to the manager of Ford Motor Company Global Brand Licensing Office. My email had nothing more than a two-paragraph description of my idea and a picture of me in front of my house in Florida standing with my four 1951 Ford trucks. My initial contact was to determine the process necessary to license a 1951 Ford panel truck die-cast toy. I planned to sell toys to fund the mission. Surprisingly, the manager, John Nens, responded in six minutes and assigned my project to his associate, Mark Bentley.

Whoa, I thought, *I must have struck a nerve to get such a quick response.* Mark and I connected, and he gave me some initial guidelines if there were to be a license granted for the toy and just a little conversation about funding from the charitable arm of the company, the Ford Fund.

I shared the Ford back-and-forth with Andy and sent an email to Mark and John at Ford requesting an appointment in their offices. They agreed to April 10, and Andy was coming along to help. Andy is a true marketing genius, and a chance to visit Ford Marketing and Licensing with him alongside my dream was irresistible.

When Andy and I arrived, we were greeted by Mark Bentley and given a tour of the licensing department, shown many products, and introduced to John Nens, the director.

After a generous lunch at the Ford estate, I was given the floor and began my story of how and why I had come up with the program idea. I shared my idea of developing a for-profit, for-benefit business to help people while selling die-cast toys. John Nens looked at me and said, "Paul, do you understand what you have?" I thought for moment and responded, "Well, I think I have a good idea that is going to help a lot of people. The worst that can happen is that I wind up with a few old trucks. And that is not a bad day in Kentucky."

John began to explain to me that I had a venue to solicit help and there was *no cause* for people not to help me. He said, "Who is going to look at you and say they don't want to build confidence in children and people suffering from debilitating life challenges?"

Continuing, he said, "If you can go back to Tampa and prove you can develop this program and get it off the ground, we are going to invite you back. When you come back, we will put you with the president of the Ford Fund who will possibly be in a position to give you some money to help." I was so stunned I was speechless. Andy, sensing that something intelligible needed to be said in response, filled the gap on my behalf. John concluded the meeting asking if there was anything he could do for me before we left. I asked him if he would tell Edsel Ford II that I had been there and share with him the story of my trucks. Edsel is very involved with Ford Motor heritage collectibles including the Henry Ford Museum. John said that he had forwarded my first email about my program to Edsel, and it was one of the reasons I was invited to come in.

This one significant meeting stirred an overwhelming sense and gravity of what HogStir could become. On the plane ride home, Andy and I were so excited. There was so much to be done. It warrants me saying just this way: a few short months from my first talk at the American Teach-In, I was in the corporate offices of Ford. The pace of it still boggles me a bit.

Irons in the Fire of Hope

Around the same time as the Ford meeting, I thought I better get out to California and develop my prospective relationships with Larry Wood, Larry Gertz, and Richard Graves. I was really sick of never taking vacations and always traveling alone, so I decided to invite Steve Legens of Legens Hot Rod to travel with me. Steve was one of the restoration pros I had met through all my searching for the trucks.

Just before the trip, I had been invited to a special customer evening at the Yamaha piano dealer in Tampa. My love of music and my collection were no secret to the local dealers.

They were having a presentation of a new, state-of-the-art player system and the speaker, Craig Knudsen, was the lead software engineer for Yamaha Disklavier pianos and many other Yamaha products.

After the presentation, I got the engineer aside and started talking to him. I told him I would be going to Los Angeles and Van Nuys in the coming weeks for the project I was developing for kids. He asked who I planned to see in California, and I mentioned Richard Graves at Artistry in Motion. A look of instant surprise overtook his face. One of his friends, he explained, had founded Artistry in Motion and sold it to Richard. I could hardly believe the connection. Yet, at the same time, I was not surprised at all.

The engineer said he was sure that Artistry in Motion's founder may want to talk to me about my project. He said he would call his friend, and if she had an interest, he would give her my number and she would call me. A few days later she called me and offered that if I was on my way to California that she, too, would like to meet about my project.

When Legens and I first arrived on the West Coast, our first meeting with Larry Wood at the Mattel design studio gave us a shot of momentum. It was thrilling to meet him. He began his career at the Ford Motor Company where he designed real cars. Then, in 1969 he wanted to return to California and began in the new design department of Hot Wheels, which had just been introduced in 1968. He was chief designer until his retirement in 2009 and known the world over. He exudes boundless energy, and when we met, he was still playing semi-pro volleyball. I explained our project and intent, and Larry said he would help in any way he could.

We then headed to Artistry in Motion to meet Richard Graves. The company is low-key on the outside, but once in the door you sense a charge and excitement like anything fantastic could happen any second. Richard and one of his executives met with us and we discussed the Fire Truck Funkification and came away with some great ideas.

From Artistry we traveled to a restaurant in Sherman Oaks to meet its original founder, Dina Sterr, the woman my random Yamaha connection introduced me to. Armed with a notepad and an open heart, she shared her vast experiences in special events production. That experience included being the director of entertainment for the Louisiana World's Fair, the first female producer of the NFL's Super Bowl halftime show, and the Emmy-nominated producer of the Hollywood Christmas Parade. She also worked on countless concert tours and award shows, including the Oscars where she was on the production staff. After twenty years of producing live and televised events, she and a partner shifted focus and opened the special effects company, Artistry in Motion. Under her direction, it was an instant success and quickly became one of the premier special effects companies in the entertainment industry. And there I was one degree from the Academy of Motion Picture Arts and Sciences, the Oscars, and the Emmys.

After her introduction, she began to ask me a lot of questions about myself and my program. I recounted all that I had overcome, the unlikely progress I had made, and what I planned to do. As I've mentioned, telling my story erodes my decorum and I started getting misty-eyed. As she was taking copious notes, she began to tear up too. When I had finished my story and my hopes for the program of hope and help, she looked up and said, "Do you understand you have a television series in all of this?" I had never thought of it from that angle and tucked the possibility away. The founder of AIM suggested she might help me, and that I could bounce ideas off of her. She also suggested that if I was going to do the thing with the fire truck, I had better have two of them, one for West Coast parades and the other for East Coast parades. Thankfully, I had already found a possible second fire truck.

After the Sherman Oaks meeting, Steve and I were off to Escondido to see Randy Clark, owner of Hot Rods and Custom Stuff. Randy and Steve had met at big-time car shows where they had competed with custom rods built for customers. Never had one seen the other's shop. I had been to Randy's shop, but he graciously took us on a tour for Steve's benefit. We then discussed my project and old trucks. I brought up the idea of a second fire truck and told Randy that a rare 1952 Ford F-8 open cab was fifty-eight miles away in Anza. Randy said, "Call him and let's go see it." I did and the owner agreed to meet us at the truck site.

I had to hurriedly take Steve to the San Diego airport for a flight back to Nashville then circle back to Escondido to pick up Randy. We arrived at the site before the owner and had a good chance to walk around it in the fading light. It had been listed on eBay several times but never sold. It was a very rare truck but needed a lot of work. After all the movement and momentum of the previous weeks and the recent meetings, I had come to expect things to happen almost instantly. It was like doors were swinging open to my dream like automatic entrances at the grocery store.

The truck owner arrived, and as we ambled around the monster, I explained my program concept to the owner while he explained the pros and cons of this machine that had sat in the same spot for twenty years. The truck had spent its whole life in San Diego County first serving in the Navy and then passing through the hands of one collector before it got to him. Instead of the truck just sitting there, I wanted to put it to a more noble use again, something befitting its potential.

After that awkward time that always just precedes a conversation about money, the owner asked me what I thought of the truck and if I would be interested in it. I looked at him and asked, "Do you understand what my program is all about?"

"Yes," he replied, "the mission is to build confidence and courage in people who suffer from physical, mental, and emotional challenges."

I looked him square in the eyes and said, "How about you have some confidence in me today and give me this truck?" It was a bold question, I'll admit that. And I had a little reticence in the asking. But the belief in my program and my endless drive to see it happen opened up new vistas of boldness in me. I simply let the question hang in the air—no politeness or disclaimers. I once heard a great saying; let people feel the weight of you. If you have a noble cause or a great dream, it will compel people to do something extraordinary.

And on that day, the extraordinary happened. He gave me the fire truck for one dollar—one measly, crumpled, old dollar I had wadded in my pocket. Like so many times before, I could hardly believe it. And yet, I had no trouble believing it.

Along with the nearly free truck, I was beyond encouraged to have found so many people in positions of influence, people who could offer actual help and dollars to this dream, people who believed in the inherent goodness of what I was called to build. Two weeks later, Randy took a flatbed trailer to retrieve the beast we nicknamed Popeye. After twenty years of sitting in the same spot, it still had air in the tires and the brakes worked!

8

There Will Always Be Resistance

So much momentum had built around the program with new connections and possible partners who wanted to be a part of the amazing story of helping others. Simply by having a dream I found myself one degree from production studios, the Ford Fund, creative firms, media consultants, individuals who were and are icons in their industries, three billionaires, and new friends who would share my vision. They were all like pieces of a puzzle that I had once scattered on a tabletop but now had their specific places. The picture was coming together. All I needed to do was put them in place and a beautiful picture would emerge. At least, that's what I would see in my daydreaming. And I knew in my soul that it was true.

There's this guy named Stephen Pressfield who wrote a book *The War of Art.* In it he talks about the concept of resistance, the surge of opposition that arises to stop any life-affirming venture. Whether you're a writer, artist, entrepreneur, parent, whatever, Pressfield believes that you will encounter resistance to your beautiful vision ever being realized. I'm walking proof that his theory is true.

As the budding program exerted its gravitational pull on potential partners, a strong surge of resistance welled up from my life. Part of it was external, stuff I couldn't control. And some of it was self-inflicted. Pressfield was beyond right.

The War

The following weeks in the spring of 2007 were really busy as I prepared to move to Nashville, continued the effort to sell my other properties, find storage for my trucks, and keep my acquisitions pipeline full for much-needed income.

The Steiner assignment had borne nothing over the six month engagement but a small retainer and reimbursement of out-of-pocket expenses. Out of all the companies I had developed for Steiner acquisition, only Steve Kitt's CCMT had been engaged in a letter of intent to be acquired. My income prospects began to look abysmal.

One positive thing, though, was that I had been released to contract with other acquisitions clients. I did just that with a large equity firm named Sterling Partners. You would be unfamiliar with their company name but you will recognize one of their brands, Sylvan Learning. The new assignment seemed very promising with tens of millions in available capital and thousands of potential acquisition targets. Further, Sterling has a spectacular reputation, and they met all of my rules of starting an acquisitions relationship. They wouldn't send me on a wild goose chase or only put their toe in the water. I began to prospect for them at the same time I was moving to Nashville.

When Things Don't Sell Like They Should

While my income was drying up, my realty situation was an absolute mess. The closing on my big Florida house took place in June 2007, and I was on my way to Nashville to stay in an extended-stay motel until I could get things arranged.

The first time I saw the Nashville house empty it was shocking. The previous owner's clutter had covered up so many things that were now exposed. I had bought it as a tear down, but I was determined to live in it for at least a year until I got everything else sold and a plan under way for my program. The week before I took possession, a gigantic eighty-year-old elm had blown down in the backyard.

A month into the house, the worst of the worst appeared. While tearing out a rotten ceiling in the kitchen we discovered black mold—the kind of mold that had killed my friend Lamar. It wasn't active, but it didn't matter to me. This house was more than fifty years old, it had mold and the electrical system had been chewed up by squirrels in the attic. In my post-accident state, it was too much for me to handle. Needless to say, I had misjudged the investment and financial risk.

Every now and again, as I would sweep the floor or look at the felled tree, my thoughts would wander to my dad and my own legacy of money mismanagement. Some parts of living are about changing your family tree. When it came to money, that was one branch I couldn't quite trim. And I was headed for a freefall from it too.

Within five weeks of arriving in Nashville, I made the decision to move temporarily into an apartment and figure out what to do with the old house and expensive property I had just purchased. By this time the real estate market was really slowing. There was little to no action on my remaining Florida villa and Arizona property. The only out would be a deal for Sterling, but that wasn't looking likely for the time being. And that prospect got worse. The partner at Sterling to whom I answered was transferred to a project in Europe. As a result, his project with me stalled, and by September I was once again without work assignments and income.

I was becoming desperate with the pressure, so I reached out to a new realtor in Nashville. In hindsight, he must have been practiced in recognizing a sucker in trouble. I got sucked into a confidence game full of his empty promises. In early November, he took control of selling my *last* valuable property in Florida, the villa, with boastful promises of how he could move my large Nashville property in a matter of weeks. I willed myself into believing he could make it happen and accepted it as truth.

I believed so much, in fact, that I found another home that I wanted to purchase.

I know, I'm an idiot.

In retrospect, it almost seems like self-sabotage. But at the time, I thought the Hail Mary pass I was throwing would be a certain score. Still, I wouldn't be offended if you put this book down right now in disgust. I've done it myself a couple times at this point in the story.

I was in a bad place.

—

In the middle of all of this came Thanksgiving, and I have always enjoyed watching the Macy's Day Parade. I still had my big dreams for the Funkee Fire Truck and watched the parade intently to see vintage vehicles.

People, ant-sized in comparison to the balloons, held the Woody Woodpeckers, Ronald McDonalds, Shreks, and Mr. Potato Heads from perilous strings. I felt like I was on one of those balloons, full of hot air, and about to float up beyond rescuing at any moment.

As I watched the parade and thought of my plan, it dawned on me. The idea I had been calling HogStir was really all about courage and risking to take one step toward hope and help, believing that we're all one degree away from goodness. And then it dawned on me that I could anchor my idea in One Degree. It had a better ring and hook right away.

—

The new Nashville home that I shouldn't have bought December 2007, it was big. It needed modification and remodeling, and I dove into it. The realtor continued to lead me on with a string of exaggerations about my Florida and Nashville properties while he collected a commission on the house I had just purchased. I still hadn't seen even one offer. I finally pulled him off the listing, though the damage of my mis-guided belief had already been done. I hired a realtor in Tampa to handle its sale. In April 2008 it sold and closed, and I walked away after fees and mortgage settlement with a small amount of equity. I had a $325,000 hard dollar equity loss on *one* house plus I had paid out more than $100,000 in mortgage and main-tenance fees during my thirty-month ownership.

As for the Nashville property, the one I bought close to the influential neighbors, the realtor kept leading me on for months promising that a longtime friend and client was going to pay nearly a million for it. I finally had had enough of his lies and exaggerations. I later found out that he had planned to screw me on the property once I collapsed financially. My poor choices had placed me in a very vulnerable position. What a mess.

Meanwhile, in the first four months of 2008 I had prospected for consulting assignments and none were available.

As I was preparing to move to the newest Nashville home, I was doing some serious clearing and cleaning up of the land-scape surrounding the house. A small creek snaked its way through my property and others around me. One Saturday in April, I put on my high water waders and jumped in the creek to clear debris. I worked my way to the road, technically through other people's properties, and was putting limbs and trash in a dumpster that was at my house. I got to the last neighbor's home, and there was a log that was too large for me to handle by myself. I looked across the street, and there was a young man trimming some trees with a chain saw so I walked over, introduced myself, and asked him if he could help. He had a landscaping business and he was more than willing to make some money and help me. I paid him thirty-five dollars, gave him my business card, pointed to my home and told him I may need his services some time.

The following day I received a call.

"Paul, this is Jonathan. I helped you with the log yesterday."

"Yes, hi Jonathan. What can I do for you?"

"I showed your card to my mother last night, and she said she went to grade school and high school with you."

He said her maiden name was Bonnie Happel. I was floored. I grew up in a town of 250 people where everyone knew one another or we were even related by blood. Bonnie and I were not related; but we had the same first cousins through marriage. I had always joked that if you didn't know someone in my hometown just say, "Hi, Cousin" because they probably were. I had not seen her in nearly thirty-eight years. We talked on the phone and in a matter of days met for dinner. There was so much to talk about, our hometown where her mother still lived, our lives since Crestwood. Cleaning up a creek and there I was one degree from a childhood friend! There was so much to rejoice in the reconnection. But within a matter of days and months, I grew to realize God had put me in that creek to find Jonathan and Bonnie.

Two days later, on a Sunday morning, I got in my panel truck and drove out to nearby Leiper's Fork. Sometimes the most relaxing thing you can do is get in your car and get out of dodge. Leiper's Fork is a genuine country community with a main street, some shops, rolling hills, farms, horses munching grass, and a palpable sense that it doesn't give a rip about the busyness the rest of us have gotten ourselves into. It is truly a beautiful gem. There's also a locally famous store there named Puckett's, a country store where you can buy groceries or sit at a food counter for homemade cookin'. It was the perfect place for me to disconnect from my turbulence.

I sat at the counter and started talking, exchanging life stories with a man who was by himself. As I was preparing to leave, a man sitting with his wife at the counter nearby stood up and said he had overheard the conversation and wanted to talk to me. He handed me his card and said he was an executive producer for a video production company. And he asked to meet for lunch. The story he overheard, he said, was the kind of stuff Oprah shows are made of.

We met a few days later. We talked about my business model and the broad plans I had to help people. He was very sensitive to my story. I was finding all too often that most people are one degree from some version of the suffering I have experienced or personal challenges I manage. Both of his sons had served in Iraq and both have severe Post-Traumatic Stress Disorder problems. He invited me to meet with the owners of his company and with another media consulting company.

We got together the following Wednesday at the SESAC building on Music Row. The meeting went well, and the owners of his company were engaged and wanted to participate. The following day all of us were to meet with the media consultants with whom they were aligned. It was May 8, and my friend who had introduced me to Propeller Consulting in Franklin, Tennessee wanted to attend the meeting. It happened to be raining that day, and he offered to drive since I didn't like getting my panel truck out on the wet roads. At the time, it was a purely nice gesture that would turn sour.

We got down to Music Row early and had some lunch before our meeting. The drive to the media consultant's office was less than two-tenths of a mile, so I slid in the car and did not buckle up. It was a stupid decision and one that would cost me dearly. The pouring rain was loud on the windshield as we pulled up behind the first car stopped by the traffic light. The office entrance was just yards away. The light turned green, and we accelerated. The car in front of us, however, had not begun to move and we rear ended them with a force you wouldn't expect from a car just starting to move. I was thrown headfirst into the spot where the overhead lining and windshield meet. It wasn't the first time I'd hit my head.

—

It was a Saturday in the fall of 1987, and though I loved being neighborly, I didn't particularly care to climb up Mr. Wood's tree that morning to trim some branches. Still, he was older, and I knew he would like some company and to feel a sense of industry around his yard. After a quick glass of orange juice for breakfast, I stepped out on the covered porch, and there was Clark waiting for me. He was wearing tired pajamas and house shoes, ready to inspect my work.

I walked over and said good morning, and he explained

what needed doing. I grabbed the ladder he'd gotten out of his mess of a garage, leaned it against the tree, and began climbing with one hand on the ladder rungs and the other holding a chain saw.

From the ground, the branches he pointed out seemed like child's play. It felt like I could've nearly jumped and reached them. But from the ladder leaning high up against the tree, the ground seemed to have dropped out, like it was in the bottom of a cloud-covered chasm. I had to steel myself against tiny fears. I wanted to get this Samaritan deed done so I could go about my day.

With Mr. Wood half watching, half patrolling the street with suspicious eyes, my first cuts began to make their way to the ground below like artful snips from a barber's chair.

With the minor trimming work done to clear space for the chain saw, I cranked it up and began to zing through the wood. It was a pretty big branch, and I was being immensely careful. Power tools plus height should not be taken lightly. I was nearly finished cutting the branch when its outstretched weight and the power of gravity began pulling down its one final connection on the tree. Before I could cut it through-and-through, the branch swung like a pendulum with the fibrous wood bending and cracking. That pendulum hit my ladder, and I tottered back and forth. I threw the chain saw away from me as I plunged fifteen feet to the concrete sidewalk below. The only thing that saved my life was breaking the fall with my arms. Somehow no bones were broken, but there was instant head trauma. I was beat up from that for more than two years.

Four years later, I was thrown from a horse. I had a right nasty frontal head concussion. My short term memory was busted for a week, which is why I can't tell you more about my fall from the horse.

—

Hitting the windshield after a fender bender may not seem like a big deal. But my head already had its fair share of collisions. That small accident reached back into history and called up a sudden and excruciating head and neck trauma. I knew I was in trouble. We went to the meeting anyway, but after a few minutes of trying to keep it together, I had to admit I was in too much pain. We went to the emergency room where I had a CT scan. My vital signs were taken, and I was told I had stroke-level blood pressure. I did not have blood pressure problems before the accident. I was released and told to see my primary care physician about my blood pressure. My friend and I returned to the BMI headquarters where I met with the consultants and explained the program. Hours later I was very, very sick.

Over the weekend I tried to deal with the pain using medicine, but I got sicker and sicker with vomiting. I had feelings of vertigo if I bent over. I was in trouble. I went back to the emergency room the following Monday and had another CT scan. It showed a severe concussion and still stroke-level blood pressure. I was reassured by the medical staff I would be okay, but I needed to get to my primary care physician about the blood pressure. Promptly.

Flirting with the "Family Badge"

I made an appointment with my primary care physician and we began a medication regimen to bring the blood pressure down. Over the next four weeks and adjusting medications it still persisted, even though I had a resting heart rate of only 58. Finally my doctor suggested that I take a treadmill stress test. The test required that I get to a heart rate of 148 within eight minutes but it took eleven. Two days later I was in front of a cardiologist, Dr. Gina Chandler, who saw a blip at the end of the stress test and was concerned by what she saw. Even though I had maintained a ninety-five pound weight loss after my gastric bypass surgery, I could not outrun my family's genetic disposition to heart disease or my previous unhealthy lifestyle. I was praying for the best but fearing the worst. The day after a cardio scoring and a CT scan, I received a call from the doctor's office that I was to come back in immediately. This could not be good news.

As I sat in front of Dr. Chandler, she calmly tried to prepare me for what was to come. I looked over at her medical degree on the wall while her voice faded away, and I imagined the face of my mother in that frame. She had the same sympathetic face as the day when my dad fell on our living room floor with his heart attack, the day I ran up from the basement. She told me that a cardio scoring of 0–200 was acceptable but mine was 1,480. I melted with fear in the chair. Finally, all of my family pain and suffering with heart disease, catalyzed by the car accident, had found me. She went on to tell me that I needed to have a heart catheterization immediately to determine the risk, that I was about to deal with a pending health crisis, either heart attack or stroke. She also talked about doing stents if she could during the catheterization procedure. I couldn't bear to listen and began to sweat with fear. Drenched, I made an appointment for my heart catherization.

Just three weeks before my heart diagnosis, I had contracted with the media consulting group that came from the Puckett's producer to develop the One Degree business model. With my business income faltering, my real estate equity vanishing and my debt gobbling my cash, I had to make a difficult choice. I could pursue the program down to my last dollar or give up and pay my mortgages on properties that would never recover the original investment. This time the stakes were real and down to the last dime. Then divine intervention. The $100,000 plus that was to have been paid after the closing sale of AMI, Inc. in 2004 had gotten caught in litigation between the buyer and Lamar's estate. Here it is nearly four years later, and after settlement between parties, I received enough money between that payment and my remaining total cash to pay the $85,000 fee for the One Degree business and branding development.

One of the people in the consulting group is a guy named Ned, a nationally recognized PR specialist and author. During a phone call to plan for our upcoming meeting, Ned asked me to tell him about the book I was writing. I rattled off a few topics, including the story about my gastric bypass surgery.

Ned interrupted, "My brother-in-law is an internationally recognized bariatric surgeon who pioneered some technology and techniques that have become the gold standard."

"My surgeon is well known too. I bet your brother-in-law knows him. His name is Dr. Alan Wittgrove."

"My God," Ned gasped. "Alan is my brother-in-law."

I had my heart catheterization on July 3. As they wheeled me into the operating room for the procedure, and as I lay under the big light, I thought of my family and all they had endured with their heart health, challenges, and deaths. It was as if my dad, mom, and brother walked beside my hospital bed holding on to the rails and holding my hands as I watched ceiling tiles pass like highway lines at night. They whispered encouragement in my ear—but all of us only half-believed it. One recess of my soul knew that my time had come, that I would be joining my parents.

They wheeled me through big swinging doors. I thought for a moment how effortlessly they opened and closed. A team was waiting, expressionless behind their masks, with sterile hands and businesslike postures. Then the oxygen mask. Then the counting backwards. Then . . .

It was done, and I was back in my room, bloated and groggy. Time in a hospital is not like real time. It moves so slowly, like your own personal time capsule with history zooming past. I tuned my attention to my chest and tried to feel what was going on in there. *Was the catheterization successful? Are there stents?* Then the door handle clicked—the most exciting thing to happen in hours—and Dr. Chandler came through and sat down next to my bed. "Stents are not an option," she informed me, "and you need as many as five heart bypasses, and soon."

"Doctor," I said, "I think I'd prefer to die." With all that had happened in the weeks and months leading up to surgery, I was tired in my very marrow. I couldn't conjure the strength and the will to go through this. I knew what my family had been through, I knew the ending, and I couldn't act like it wasn't my fate.

"Well, Mr. Wittwer. I am going to leave you in this bed until you come up with a better idea."

I looked at her the way any adult would when he's spoken to like a child. She read the annoyance and disbelief on my face.

"You can do it." She paused, looking me straight in the eyes. "And you must."

And with that, she put her hands on her knees, hoisted herself off the chair, patted my hand, smiled, and left.

Witch, I thought. But deep down I was thankful I hadn't died already.

How on Earth?

When a star uses up all its energy and heads toward a certain death, it gets much bigger. I don't know why, I'm not a scientist. But once the star is all bloated, it finally collapses on itself and creates a black hole, the most inescapable force known to man.

The moment you receive a diagnosis and must undergo a

life-threatening surgery to resolve a life-threatening disease, everything goes black. It is the darkest moment of the darkest hour of your life. I felt completely alone and helpless. The Family Badge I had dreaded for so long would soon be mine too. My gastric bypass surgery was elective, and I reflected on the wonderful quality of life and health it had given me. There was no real choice for this new diagnosis. Without the surgery, I could face things much worse than death, strokes, and heart attacks.

My situation felt like a dying star.

When I was eighteen I decided that I would never have children because I did not want them to experience all of the pain that I had experienced in my family when my parents became sick and challenged. I was convinced that I would be just like my parents, that I would be faced with health and money challenges. My time had come, and I reflected on the Colonel's life. How would he get through this?

Harland Sanders had three children with his first wife, Josephine, to whom he was married for thirty years, two daughters, Mildred and Margaret, and a son, Harland Sanders Jr. In 1930, Harland Jr. died of an infection at age twenty. The Colonel was forty, and how did he choose to deal with the bereavement and loss of his son? Harland Sr. reflected on all of the hardship he had endured between the ages of twenty and forty and found solace in knowing Harland Jr. would never have to know such pain. For me, the children I never had were never confused and hurt by my ups and downs, losses, mental challenges or sickness. I found comfort in this.

I lay there in the hospital bed taking stock of all that I had to overcome. Funding several mortgages, home repairs, hiring the media consultants, and my experience with Lamar years before. The values of my properties had evaporated. How on earth was I going to overcome heart surgery, recover, and try to make a living?

I had one active hope. I was banking everything on the business plan being prepared for One Degree—everything. The only other long shots were the CCMT deal closing for Steiner and/or my disability insurance that I had been funding for more than two decades with a company named UNUM. In 1986, after my brother had his first heart surgery combined with his mental illness diagnosis in 1984, he was uninsurable for disability income insurance. I was thirty-four years old and had my small consulting practice for less than four years. The thought of being sick and without income was jarring. All of us have a one-in-three chance of becoming disabled in our lifetimes. I thought about all of the sickness in my family and made the decision to purchase disability insurance January 1, 1987, and throughout its term increase the benefit every time the option was available to me. I bet against my family health history.

No matter if those two options worked out, I was still probably going to have to file bankruptcy. If you think it is tough to take on a life-risking medical crisis and surgery, take it on knowing you have no income and resources to sustain you when and if you survive it.

An hour had passed since Dr. Chandler left me on my own to come up with a better idea. My EMDR therapy of seven years before helped me manage that first hour. It had desensitized me to many of the traumas and images related to illness in my family. While I had a real *hellstorm* ahead of me, I had to put my mind on someone else and who better than the Colonel?

When Harland was ten years old, his family of four were desperately poor. His father had died two months before Catherine was born. It was 1900 and his mother worked in a tomato canning factory while trying to make ends meet as a seamstress. A neighboring farmer needed help clearing land all by hand, so she hired Harland out to the farmer for two dollars a month and board. Off he went. After a month, the neighbor returned Harland to his mother refusing to pay the two dollars because Harland had only cleared one acre. His mother scolded him so mercilessly that he made up his mind that he would never again take on a job he could not complete or in which he could not excel. His only excuse, he had spent too much time watching squirrels and butterflies.

A second painfully slow hour had passed since Dr. Chandler had left the room. I will admit I can become my own worst company at times. This was one of those times. I drifted back to family for a moment cursing how I'd been born into the shallow end of the gene pool. Just as I had drifted back to family, the Colonel drifted back to me to speak through his life.

In 1911, Harland had settled in Jeffersonville, Indiana just across the river from Louisville, Kentucky. At the time there were only two means to move between the cities, a distant K&I railroad bridge in New Albany or directly across from Jeffersonville on a wooden hull, sternwheeler ferry boat that couldn't run in the winter due to risk of sinking from ice. It was unreliable at best in the spring or fall due to rising waters and the risk of being sunk by floating logs. Everyone referred to the boat as "Old Asthma" because it sounded like it wheezed when running. The operators of the ferry insisted they had a perpetual franchise from the government to be the exclusive ferry operator between the cities.

Harland didn't believe the franchise story and went to the Louisville library for ten days to research the question and found there was no such thing. He discovered the opportunity he was looking for, build a steel hulled ferry boat that could run in many river conditions. He shared his knowledge of the opportunity with a few Jeffersonville businessmen and together formed a ferry boat company—with nothing more than a promise to build the boat and sold stock in the company for $62,000 in thirty days. The boat cost $40,000 to build and in 1912 Harland christened it the *Froman M. Coots*, named for a prominent local funeral director. It crossed the river until the end of World War II. Harland pocketed the other $22,000 as commission for his salesmanship. He was not yet twenty-two years old. To give you a sense of the scale of this wealth, a 1912 Ford Model T cost $600 twice the annual average income for an American worker.

Three and a half hours had passed, now I was convinced Dr. Chandler had left me there to detox my pessimism. It was working as the Colonel lent his hand. I had made a commitment to see my project through regardless of what it may extract. I had to take stock in myself and realize I still had my greatest resource—me! I had only imaginations of where I would get money to start over. Just like Harland and his ferry boat I had a ferry boat of a different kind I wanted to build to help people get to the other side of their troubled waters. First I would have to pray to God to pilot me across my own.

Now I just had to get through heart surgery!

When Dr. Chandler finally came back *four hours later*, I had a different perspective.

"Okay, let's do it," I said

She smiled, made a check with a flick of her pen on the clipboard, never said a word, and walked out.

The Hospital, Again

On July 16, Bonnie delivered me to the hospital for surgery. She patiently waited until there was no need to wait any longer. I was alone, and I was afraid until I remembered what my mother had told me about her heart surgery in 1975. She was comforted by the presence of the Lord, so I began to silently pray. I closed my eyes and prayed to God to see me through this and for a safe recovery. I had a team of nine people working on my One Degree program, and I did not want to let them down. I also prayed to make it through because I *knew* there would be people on the other side of my surgery who would need encouragement when they have similar struggles. I needed to pray for myself too. I was going into heart surgery with $250 in cash left to my name, health insurance in place to deal with the surgery, a prepaid week in respite care at an assisted living facility while I owed $1,600,000. When there was nothing left to say, I called the anesthesiologist back in and it was lights out.

I awoke hours later at two in the morning in recovery to the sounds of heart monitors beeping and nurses shuffling. It was a sterile environment, and I searched for something to drink. I found the nurse call button and let it rip. A nurse quickly appeared and asked, "What can I do for you, Mr. Wittwer?"

"I desperately need a Diet Coke." I replied. While I don't smoke, drink, or chase women, I will confess I have a Diet Coke addiction. We all have something.

With a smile and a wink of her eye she said, "Well you have survived heart surgery, I guess you deserve one!"

You would think they turned me into part robot what with all the tubes, the temporary pacemaker, IVs, and telemetry hooked up to me. I guess my surgery was sort of like a reboot. Hours passed as I dozed in and out. At six thirty in the morning, a heavyset nurse walked into my room, looked at my chart, and said, "Mr. Wittwer I see where you have had gastric bypass surgery. I had the surgery in January and have lost eighty-five pounds. I have eighty more to go. But I am having a few challenges. Can I ask you for some ideas that can help me?"

I had been awake for a few short hours and already my prayers had been answered. I was already helping someone. We talked about post-operative gastric bypass care and the choices that worked best for me. She told me that her husband was serving in Iraq, and he had not seen her since her weight loss surgery. She wanted to have it all off before he got home. To this day I imagine their reuniting and how incredible it must've been for them both.

In a matter of hours, I was moved to the cardiac care floor where the hard work was about to begin. The first thing they tell you is that you have to get out of the bed and start moving. The very first thing I wanted to do was stand in front of the mirror in the bathroom. I had to see the scar. I shuffled across the sterile linoleum and approached the bathroom door at snail speed. I reached out my hand and clicked the knob. A light automatically came on. There I stood, looking like death itself with frizzed hair and droopy eyes. I felt terrible. My body was swollen and distended from the anesthesia. I slowly brought both my hands to the lapels of my robe and pulled them back. There it was, the scar, tender and pulsating. I could sense it moving in and out like the lazy bubbling of volcanic lava. I now had the Family Badge.

Bonnie was there for me every day, and soon it was time for her to transport me for my week of recovery. Prior to the surgery, despite all the properties I owned, there wasn't one—not a one—where I could take care of myself. So, I made reservations at an assisted living facility. When we arrived, I walked in under my own power, and Bonnie and the staff got me settled. Over the next few days I would grow to know some of the residents. The youngest resident was eighty and they stretched up to nearly one hundred. Except for me, that is, I was the youngest person there. I gained inspiration from the residents: if they could keep going at their age, then I could get over heart surgery.

There is one gem of a woman from whom I gained the most inspiration, a Japanese American nearly ninety years old, bent over from the ravages of scoliosis and a stroke that left her with a brace on both her right arm and leg. She slowly ambled through the halls on a walker and can only look to her left when speaking to you. This very same woman was the personal secretary and translator for General Douglas MacArthur. She can still say plenty in the five languages she knows. And what's more, with full use of her left arm and partial use of her right, she uses her computer to make birthday cards for all of the residents. Seeing her determination, I knew anything was still possible for me.

Can I Get Off the Roller Coaster, Please?

I felt markedly better after my recovery week, and I finally returned to my own home with my new challenges. I had cardio therapy three days a week for three months. During my heart surgery my neck was hyper-extended, and I was having severe neck pain. I also had physical therapy three days a week for two months to help the neck injury caused by the Music Row crash and exacerbated by my surgery. It was during physical therapy that I discovered a problem with my right shoulder. An MRI revealed that I had suffered a partial tear of my rotator cuff during heart surgery, and it was inflamed by a bone spur.

You would think I had seen enough of doctors by this point, but on December 2, I had to have surgery on my shoulder. After

I had completed all of the other physical therapies, I had more! During the recovery for my right shoulder, my left rotator cuff began to fail, and it would require cortisone shots every six weeks and extensive physical strengthening throughout 2009.

———

For five months, for every doctor's appointment and physical therapy visit, I sat in the waiting area of Premier Orthopedics. In the lobby, a television loops one channel for AccentHealth. The programming is all about health-related wellness, quality of life, and medical procedures and cures. The hosts of the programming are Robin Meade and Dr. Sanjay Gupta of CNN. Maybe I got a little brainwashed because of how often I saw that station, but I would eventually visit the AccentHealth website. For months I kept thinking about how I would take the base business model of AccentHealth and embellish it with One Degree life stories of overcoming. My instincts kept telling me there was some kind of business partnership there, yet I never made a call to them.

———

The months following heart surgery were really tough. One sneeze could ruin my day. I was on my own at the house and Bonnie checked in on me constantly. My neighbors were supportive too. I was waiting on the One Degree business plan to be completed, but the gravity of my financial situation was really starting to weigh me down. I was no longer able to pay my mortgages or any bills. I was going to have to start liquidating my possessions. The phone began to ring with creditor calls.

The One Degree plan was completed in mid-November while I was still gaining my physical strength but losing my financial standing. At the same time I was watching the world financial meltdown. You learn as a recovering heart patient that you have to avoid stress, yet I was buried in it. I had hired a truly professional team with years of national and international media experience. I was excited to get the plan but overwhelmed by how expensive the initial start-up cost would be as they envisioned it.

Starting a for-profit for-benefit media company is a very expensive process. It would take a lot of resources to capture the true stories of people who have overcome their challenges to become who they are and then serve that up as hope and help for the viewer. The plan entailed a television series, micropublishing for books, ecommerce, publishing the book you are reading now, and a website with social networking. I wanted to do all of this to provide hope, help, and courage to people in need and give the profits away.

Outlined over a 175-page document, with a price tag of fourteen million dollars, my heart sank when I first got the packet. Good grief. With my experience in mergers and acquisitions, and looking at the world crisis, I knew immediately this would be nearly impossible.

I quickly contacted local Nashville area venture capital firms and got the package to them. I also Googled "media venture capital" for money source leads. The first search revealed

M/C Ventures. I quickly scanned their website and portfolio of investments, and there it was: AccentHealth. They had purchased the company in September 2008. I called the firm's office and got the phone number of the person overseeing the AccentHealth investment. After a quick elevator pitch, he agreed to review my plan. I shipped it out immediately before Thanksgiving. And there I was, one degree from the capital I needed for my plan the whole time I sat in physical therapy watching AccentHealth.

In the meantime, I met with bankruptcy attorneys. They were bleak meetings. There were no buyers for my properties, a world financial meltdown, mounting bills, and no income in sight to pull me out of my nosedive. I was advised to file Chapter 7 liquidation whereupon I would be allowed to have a total of less than four thousand dollars in assets excluding exempt retirement accounts. And there I was, one degree from financial abyss.

But my plan, hopes, and dreams for One Degree were still intact and unassailable. From the beginning of the concept, I had been willing to go down to my last dime. I had surrendered to this, God's plan for my life.

———

Three days after my shoulder surgery, my cell phone rang. It was one of the managers of the AccentHealth portfolio account with M/C Ventures.

"Paul, do you have some time to talk to us?" he asked. "We have been through your complete package and have a few questions." A few minutes turned into nearly an hour as we not only discussed the business plan but my life, personal challenges, and overcoming.

It was clear from our conversation that they wanted to believe in me, and they shared my passion and vision. They invited me to continue the conversation after the first of the year, starting with a conference call to go over the model and financials. I had no idea where this would lead. But after the months of surgeries, therapy, and recovery, I was eager to shift my energies to the program. Granted, I was liquidating all of my possessions while I was looking for an injection of capital, but hope and help were coming for me.

Deep down, I wanted to believe I was doing what the Colonel would have done.

9

Finding Your One Degree

I got out of the shower one morning in December 2008 and looked at myself in the mirror. I thought of the handout I had given Mrs. Lash's sixth grade class—the kitten looking in the mirror and the lion staring back. I think I had been seeing myself somewhere in between. Not helpless, certainly. But not the king of the jungle either. Maybe I needed a dose of my own medicine. I looked myself dead in the eye and reminded my reflection, "What matters most is how you see yourself."

When I lost my weight in 2003 after my surgery, I had a washboard stomach, a novelty for a guy who grew up always between chubby and fat. Now I was getting a little baggy again from lack of attention. The Family Badge seemed less angry, the pulsating red had faded to an ember orange. The sites from my gastric bypass faded. I had gained eight pounds since my move to Nashville, running a short yo-yo between 170 and 177. My waist had inched up to a 33/34, and it bothered me.

With all the gazing at my body, I realized I was not looking at the most important thing—my spirit. It wasn't my body that pulled me through the dark days of my PTSD therapy, living at Walmart, building wealth, and then losing it all. I looked in the mirror again and thought about all of the experiences I had had in just a few short years. I stood there speechless, tears welling in my eyes with self-doubt for the bad choices that seemed to always creep back into my world. I was reaching deep within my soul to try to find personal grace and forgiveness.

In all of the work I had done with Dorney, I had learned that the only way to progress and recover from your mistakes is to be honest with yourself and others. The truth is, when I lived at Walmart, I had a lot of unfinished business within in my own heart and mind that being slim, fit, and rich didn't fix. I realized, too, that despite how my achievements hadn't rescued me the way I'd hoped, there was one consistent element that brought goodness into my life. It was the *one degree*. It was the truth that when I found myself in a moment of great need some spectacular door opened for me, or some perfect connection was made through a friend or childhood acquaintance or TV commercial. I believe my one degree experiences have something to do with the side effects of my PTSD and OCD tendencies. But the universe has to do its part too. Or I would say, God does his part too.

It dawned on me that to overcome the difficulty I was in—the impending bankruptcy, the physical recovery, the ongoing emotional recovery, and the establishment of One Degree—I would have to depend on one degree, that strange mixture of perseverance and God's grace.

Pennies on the Dollar

In November of 2008, I watched as my property across the street from Martina McBride auctioned for less than half a million when it had appraised close to three quarters of a million three months before. In January 2009, I watched as my furniture was auctioned for seventeen cents on the dollar. In February 2009, my property in Arizona was auctioned at the county courthouse for nearly one hundred thousand dollars less than the original note and a third of what I had paid for it. The bank was the only bidder to show up, by the way. Ultimately my last purchased property in Nashville was sold at a courthouse foreclosure sale in March 2010. Again the only buyer was the bank. All totaled, I lost a million dollars. It was hard-earned, after-tax money flushed down the financial sewer on four properties and their mortgages in less than twenty-nine months. There were a couple of bright spots in all of the darkness: the acquisition of Steve Kitt's school by Steiner had closed two weeks after my heart surgery, and liquidation of my collection of 1951 Ford trucks.

After all the foreclosures and liquidations, especially in the context of multiple surgeries and emotional diagnoses, you begin to learn that life is not about the stuff. Even though I had been down this road before, I was *finally* learning that life is about how you see yourself and the world around you, how you choose to move forward despite the odds and circumstances, and how you commit to the well-being of yourself and of others.

I had surrendered myself to a purpose and a plan. I simply had to keep going wherever that course would lead. I reconnected with an acquaintance I had made eighteen months before, Dan Merrell, founder and CEO of Propeller Consulting. His company focuses on marketing for faith-based products and entertainment. Dan is also an ordained minister, which gives him a unique perspective on his business and the service to his clients. Although I had chosen a different firm to prepare my business plan, Dan welcomed me with open arms and volunteered his services to help me make One Degree come alive. He believed in me and my mission straightaway and has never been less than generous with his time and immense talent. From the initial plan, Dan and his team created a smart proposal. A streamlined, aggressive plan that needed a reasonable amount of start-up capital, which was key in the flailing market of 2008. I was immediately taken by the adeptness of the group and their ability to rightsize the plan for the moment we were in economically. Dan took my 175-page business plan down to 68 pages and the start-up capital requirement from fourteen million to under a million. He also helped me focus on one the most important part of my start-up, writing this book.

All Roads Lead to Oprah

Before the New Year, I had watched dozens of trailers for *Oprah*. The New Year would see the launch of her "Best of Life" series. The trailers showed clips of Oprah talking about her own weight story, the infamous cycle she became known for before she was the mogul we know today. She would get to tough topics about the whole person—spirituality, finances, health, you name it. I made a note on my calendar to catch the shows. (Yes, I'm proud to admit it. I am an old-ish white guy who watches *Oprah*.)

One of her guests was singer Carnie Wilson who had gastric bypass surgery in 1999, lost over 180 pounds, had skin reduction surgery, and became a weight loss celebrity telling her story. After all of the adulations, Carnie fell off the wagon and ballooned back up to 220 pounds. Now there she was again on *Oprah* talking about how she was again losing weight and all that it required.

My ears were ablaze. I don't know Carnie Wilson, but I do have something very personal in common with her. We have the same bariatric surgeon, Dr. Alan Wittgrove. After watching the first three days of the series, my instincts for One Degree were in overdrive. It was public knowledge that Oprah had made a deal with Discovery Communications to take over the Discovery Health Channel and rebrand it the Oprah Winfrey Network (OWN). I believed that my story and my business may just fit with OWN, so I got on the Oprah.com website and researched all of the people she had hired to develop the new network.

I scanned the bios of the staff for the best entry point, and I spotted a Jeff Meier, Sr. VP of scheduling, acquisitions, and strategy. I knew this would be a guy I could relate to with acquisitions speak. I waited ten days to let the New Year rush pass, and then I dialed the number. I got straight through to his assistant who laughed when I told her that I was Paul Wittwer of Hogtrails. She politely took my name and number and made no promise Jeff would call me back.

Less than twenty-four hours later, however, Jeff was on my phone. Within minutes, I had his full attention and we talked for an hour. He suggested that we talk again after he completed two weeks of travel in front of him. I hung up the phone heartened.

Four days later, I called Jeff's assistant again and asked if I could get on his calendar when his travels were over. She let me know that he was going to be in Las Vegas the following week for a three-day conference of the National Association of Television Production Executives (NATPE). I had no idea what NATPE was before I talked to her, but during the call I looked it up online and casually said to her that I had been thinking about going to the conference myself. Yes, it was a little white lie, I confess. But hey, I was a determined soul on a mission. I asked if I could get an appointment with Jeff at NATPE. At this point, I didn't even know if I could attend the conference. After hanging up with Jeff's assistant, I instantly called the NATPE folks to find out.

They had closed their online registration weeks back, and I had to sweet talk my way in. Also, the only available money I had came from the proceeds of my ongoing liquidations. I negotiated a discounted fee for the conference and booked a room in the cheapest motel Las Vegas had to offer. Luckily I had a free round-trip ticket on Southwest to get there. Practically within the same breath where we said good-bye, I called Jeff's assistant back and told her my travel arrangements for Las Vegas. The next day, I got a call with a confirmed thirty-minute meeting.

I headed to Vegas with a few scraggly dollars in my wallet and did my best to play the part. When my thirty minutes arrived and I was face to face with Jeff, I was ready. Some thirty minutes are more important than others. This was one of them. He rushed in fresh from a meeting with NBC and gave me his full attention. I breezed through the highlights of my passion and vision, pitched One Degree, and suggested that it could be a movement appropriate for OWN. After our thirty minutes passed, he looked at me wide-eyed and said, "Paul your story is simply overwhelming. Your vision and program are important. When I get back to the office, we will set up a conference call with our other team members." Then as quickly as he came, Jeff dashed to a meeting with HBO.

Three weeks later, the conference call with Jeff and another exec at OWN took place. Dan (from Propeller) joined us for the call, and the hour flew by. Jeff also made a connection for me with a producer at Harpo Studios so that my program and eventual book—the one you're holding right now—could be routed to Oprah personally. And there I was, one degree from Oprah.

Done but Not Finished

By the end of March 2009, I had the basic manuscript for my book complete, but it was going to take time and money to get it rewritten by a professional ghostwriter and printed into galleys for review by agents and publishers. Thank God for Dan again. I knew nothing of publishing and I could only pray that I would find the right help.

In the meantime, I stayed hot on the trail of all the other warm leads that had come into my life over the last months. After the October 2008 fallout of the world economy, it looked like any available capital for start-ups like mine had vanished in the plunging stock market. I decided to approach the Nashville Capital Network (NCN), a local organization supported by venture capitalist angels. You would think in Music City, one of the three entertainment hot spots of America, there would be someone who would want to at least look at my plan. But wallets were skittish, and everyone declined. Still, I received an email that NCN was holding a panel discussion on the topic, "Financing Your Company: Bootstrapping as an Alternative to Venture Capital." One of the four panelists on the program was a guy named Clint Smith, a cofounder the Nashville-based Emma, Inc., a Web-based service company that manages email marketing and communications for more than twenty-five thousand organizations worldwide. After researching Clint's start-up, which is only seven years old and has experienced significant success, my instincts told me I needed to seek this guy out.

I arrived at the discussion purposely late and marched my way, in plain view of all the attendees and panelists, to the front row. I don't take notes but I am very attentive. During the discussion, Clint had made the comment that his greatest fear was failing and "he and his family living in a van down by the river."

I hadn't parked by a river, nor was I in a van. But I guessed that my Walmart/trailer combo would be close enough to enter an engaging conversation if I had the chance to talk to Clint.

As the panel wrapped, I had the chance I had hoped for. Before I told him anything of my program, I recalled his comment about living in a van down by the river. I shared my story of falling down financially, living at Walmart, and yet here I was standing with him talking about hope and potential. I assured him my days at Walmart had served me well. After a quick pitch for One Degree, we arranged to have coffee at Starbucks in a few days.

During our coffee, I shared most of my story with Clint. Any part of my story is hard to grasp and process for most people who have family, children, loved ones, and reasonably good health. Clint asked if I would share the most current business model and of course I agreed. A couple of weeks passed and Clint sent me an email that he wanted to introduce me to his friend, Bryan Norman, who is a senior editor for a big publisher located in Nashville. He said his friend would be interested in my story and may be able to provide some direction on my book.

My Least Becomes My Most

Despite all the momentum for my dream, the other areas of my life were less accelerated. I was living on little to nothing, going to motels that serve breakfast to have a good meal for the day to conserve what little I had. My only cash flow was from selling my possessions on Craigslist and eBay. I had months of ongoing physical therapy for my shoulder and neck and enough doctor appointments that they nearly dedicated a waiting-room chair in my name.

I had filed on my UNUM disability policy within three weeks of my heart surgery to get some much-needed money. From the moment I filed, the company and especially Rhonda Lamothe, my benefits specialist at UNUM, were working feverishly to get all of the information from doctors, hospitals, and providers in order to help me with my claim and get funds to me for my benefits. But these sorts of things never happen as quickly as you'd like them to. The weeks grew into months as my heart and subsequent shoulder surgery issues were ensnarled in the auto accident issues. I was getting desperate. That and pilfering bagels from your local Holiday Inn Express doesn't do wonders for your sense of self-worth.

I began to suffer from a sudden and severe bout of depression. From my time with Dorney, I had learned to recognize that cloud, and I knew I needed some counseling to help me through. The difficulty of the previous months had unearthed more deep-seated needs. I'll be honest and say that I thought once or twice about the Heirloom.

I told Rhonda what I was experiencing and asked if she could offer any direction. She knew of my PTSD issues from my file, and she suggested I see my primary care physician for help with my depression. Rhonda also mentioned that given all of my physical and recurring mental challenges throughout my lifetime, I should consider filing for long-term disability.

Oh, she also said that nearly a year of benefits was headed my way and that all of it would be tax free. That was incredible news, for sure, but the call felt both like a big hug (from the news about the money) and a sucker punch to the gut (from the news that I could be considered disabled).

I have learned through my hardships that putting a name on something can be empowering, but it can also be devastating. When an illness doesn't have a name, you don't have to acknowledge it exists. But when someone says you have PTSD, or you are bipolar, or you are disabled, you all of the sudden feel less capable, less adequate. You would think that I'd be used to the news by now. But dear God, when I came off of that call I was struck with raw emotions that broke me to bawling tears. At a mere fifty-seven years of age, I was considered "advanced age" and possibly disabled.

My sadness morphed into resolve, and I was going to show everyone how capable I knew myself to be by multiplying hope and true help through the program that had been entrusted to me.

The Power of Words

I met with my primary care physician who recommended a psychiatrist. I gladly accepted the referral but dreaded the thought of potentially beginning a regimen of psychotropic drugs again. I had taken some after my heart surgery because my cardiologist insisted. But they severely screwed with my brain.

Within the first five minutes of meeting the psychiatrist

and discussing my symptoms, he made an off-the-cuff diagnosis that I had bipolar disorder. Just like that. In a matter of
five minutes I had a new disease. Yay. He then went on to pre-
scribe a regimen of pills for the last ten minutes of the fifteen-
minute appointment and gave a referral to a psychologist that
works in his practice. I came out of his office devastated and not
even thinking I should check the premise of the diagnosis. I
guess I had become accustomed to having whatever disease
doctors said I have. As I left his office, the traffic sounds and
the wind joined to sound like the voice of my old school counselor who made awful pronouncements over my life. I wouldn't
have been surprised if an asparagus stalk fell from the sky and
bumped me on the head.

Some stories are worth remembering. Others are worth for-
getting. Let's just say, that my short and intense experience with
the psychiatrist was the latter. After a string of lackluster appointments with the psychologist he recommended and some apparent laziness on his part, I decided to get some different help and
a professional disability advocate to assist me with filing on
Social Security. The only good that came out of seeing this lazy
psychologist were his notes sent to Rhonda confirming what I
already knew about myself—I had unfinished business!

Building a New Path

Without a trusted counselor to turn to, I reached out to the
trusted voice of Dorney. Albeit, counseling over the phone with
someone you trust is not the same as in person, it is still better

than nothing. Dorney stood for my potential yet again. We talked about all I had accomplished since the days of September 2001 when we first started working together. He reminded me that I still have the power of choice, and that I have to choose to pull myself up as I had done before. "You have to do the work" he reminded me. "You have done it before and now you know the path. You know the energy it will require, and I am here to help if you can't find someone in Nashville in whom you can find solace and trust."

During one phone call, I was telling him about my pain every morning after pulling back the shower curtain, the part where I see my scar in the mirror.

"Dorney," I said, "every day I dread that moment because the first thing I see and look for is the Family Badge."

"Why do you do that to yourself?" he asked. "You need to put a sign on that mirror that says, 'The scar on my chest saved my life so I can enjoy the rest of it.'"

In that moment, Dorney knew exactly what I needed to hear yet again. That day the sign went on the mirror where it remains.

After speaking with Dorney, I mentioned to my new disability advocate, Vicki, that I wanted to find a female psychiatrist in Nashville who I could pay out of my own pocket without the help and bias of insurance. All Vicki knew about me was my story and information from my disability claims and intake forms. She referred me to a psychiatrist who had been successful with her other clients, and I called and made an appointment.

I know I've recounted several "coincidences" and "chance meetings" in this story. I've even given those encounters a name, "one degree." You may think it's total baloney. Or fabrications, bizarre and inconceivable. Please just hear me out.

I scheduled my first appointment with the new psychiatrist for her last appointment on a late Friday afternoon. Within fifteen minutes, we discovered that we both grew up in the same rural county in Kentucky and went to the same high school. She knew the street where I grew up. That first one-hour appointment turned into two and half hours. Suffice it to say, under her tutelage, my recovery has accelerated. She has also straightened out the lousy diagnosis I got at the last doctor. I learned I am not bipolar but still suffer from and will have off-shoot symptoms and lifetime management of my Post-Traumatic Stress Disorder.

My Guardian Angels

When everything seemed impossible and after months of working together on my disability claim, my UNUM benefits representative, Rhonda, and UNUM Insurance have delivered on every promise they made on my twenty-three-year-old policy. More important she has helped direct me through all of the hurdles to get the benefits I deserve. Yet there was a greater service she would provide. In telling me that I qualified for long-term benefits, Rhonda made me promise that I would use the money to take care of myself because my accrued benefits ensured that I would no longer have to work. Imagine that, someone I had never met, who works for an insurance company in which I had entrusted my future life risk was asking me to *promise* that I would take care of *me*! It was if she had reached out her hand to touch me, as Ann had done the day I planned to use the Heirloom.

I have kept my promise to Rhonda. After pulling myself back from the abyss, I got a solid plan together with my Nashville psychiatrist and began, once again, to do the work. Here are the elements. To deal with my social anxiety and isolation issues I started taking dancing lessons. I have taken piano lessons at the local Yamaha dealer. Most important, managing mental illness is about managing the whole body, so with input from my psychiatrist, I assembled a team to help me.

I employed the services of a personal trainer initially six days a week to bring my body back to the level of the MiniMe summer and to give me a plan for lifetime strength. I engaged Nan Allison, a registered dietician and nutritionist with a national reputation, to help me rediscover cooking, meal planning, and journaling based on my needs as a gastric bypass patient. I joined the YMCA and got back in the pool for water aerobics and am now taking swimming lessons so I can have a heart-healthy sport I can do the rest of my life. At the behest of my psychiatrist, I have developed a family of friends inside and outside of church and the YMCA and that family is growing. I will never appear on *Dancing with the Stars* or perform in Carnegie Hall, but I will at least have the nerve to ask someone to dance and not step on her feet. Oh yes, I am back to my thirty-two-inch waist and can do dozens of push-ups off the floor!

At the suggestion of my cardiologist and my psychiatrist, I will never be able to go back to the high-stakes game of mergers and acquisitions. It made me too much of an adrenaline junkie, fed my mental illness and compulsive tendencies. I have also put an excellent team of financial advisors around me to organize and manage the One Degree business, and my personal financial affairs. No more frivolity for me.

I find it all ironic that after everything I have owned and earned, I am now living in a small but comfortable apartment tastefully decorated with little furniture, my old family player piano, and driving the 2002 Jeep Liberty that I once towed behind my motorhome. I will probably be in "credit jail" the rest of my life and have no desire to ever own a home again. My promise to Rhonda also helped me to be better prepared for the stress of filing Chapter 7 bankruptcy in December 2009. All of my debts were discharged effective March 25, 2010.

Fortunately, my disability income and my retirement are exempt assets and could not be taken from me by the bankruptcy court. Amidst all this, what would appear to be the very least in my life of the past eight years has become the very most. I am gaining peace with who I am, the management of my many challenges, means and ways to develop lasting friendships, and attending church regularly. Most important *I am alive*!

The Colonel and One Degree

Here I am at a new starting point, much like the Colonel when he started out with his $105 Social Security check, recipe, and a dream. I have emerged from bankruptcy debtless, my recipe and dream for One Degree intact now funding its start on *my* disability income. Fresh and ready.

To give myself a reality check, I decided to once again refresh my vision against that of the life and times of the Colonel. In particular I wanted to discover if the Colonel Harland Sanders Charitable Foundation established in 1965 after he sold the company was still in operation and gifting today. I searched the Internet and could not find a website for the foundation, only snippets of news about gifts over time. I found one as recent as 2009 of more than $1,000,000 to a children's hospital in Birmingham, Alabama. It was still active, and I had to find out more detail, so I called the corporate offices of KFC in Louisville, Kentucky. I was directed to Cynthia Harbin, who I did not know then, is Executive Director of the KFC Foundation.

I explained to Ms. Harbin how the Colonel had impacted my life and I simply wanted to find a director of the Colonel's Foundation, which is separate from KFC, so that I could speak with them to become current on its history for my book and program plan.

"Mr. Wittwer, you need only to call Shirley Topmiller, right here in Louisville. She is on the board of the Colonel's Foundation." Ms. Harbin gave me Ms. Topmiller's phone number, and our conversation continued as she asked me questions about my book and program plan.

As our conversation wrapped up I asked, "Ms. Topmiller's name sounds very familiar. Was she at one time on the Board of KFC?"

With a slight chuckle she replied, "No, Paul, Ms. Topmiller had a far more important role in the company. She was the Colonel's personal secretary for the last twenty-eight years of his life. When you get your book finished, send me a copy."

In the instant of a phone call I was about to be within one degree of the Colonel.

My first and subsequent conversations with Ms. Topmiller have been delightful. The Colonel's Foundation has never solicited outside money. Instead it perpetuates itself and its giving off of the "Original Recipe." She confirmed many of the things I remembered about the Colonel as I shared with her his impact on my life. As my story would have it, Ms. Topmiller was responsible for making and executing the Colonel's funeral arrangements. It was because of Shirley that I was able to spend fifteen minutes with him in December 1980. Fifteen minutes that became an important part of my life story and success. She also confirmed that to his dying day the Colonel prayed to God for forgiveness for his cussin' as it disappointed his mother so. Harland often said, "Never be remembered as the richest man in the cemetery."

I sojourn on developing the One Degree business plan. My goal was, from the very beginning, to use this book as a tool, a way to get people engaged in my story so they could see the negative impact of all the maladies countless people experience every day and to give them a way to help or find hope and help for themselves. As One Degree continues to grow and take shape, I invite you to be a part of it. Maybe that means giving someone five dollars, maybe it means praying, or telling a friend you know that suffers from life's challenges that there is hope and help available. Extend yourself to help them find courage to meet, conquer, or manage their challenge. For in an instant you could become the one in need of the same. Or, perhaps you can see the one degree "coincidences" in your own life and now understand them to be the revolution of hope and help that are coming for us all.

We all have so many opportunities in this life to fail and succeed. I'm no stranger to both paths. I went from mouthing a shotgun barrel to becoming a millionaire, from believing I could be nothing to discovering a true purpose and mission for my life. At the end of the day, there are two things that emerge that can have eternal significance: how you see yourself and how you commit to helping others. You are one degree from a beautiful self-image, a beautiful friend, a beautiful life. You are also one degree from helping someone else receive those same gifts. Because hope and help are always closer than you think.

Afterword

We grow great by dreams. All big men are dreamers. They see things in the soft haze of a spring day or in the red fire of a long winter's evening. Some of us let these great dreams die, but others nourish and protect them, nurse them through bad days till they bring them to the sunshine and light which come always to those who sincerely hope that their dreams will come true.

—WOODROW WILSON

The day I graduated from the University of Kentucky, May 11, 1974, my parents gave me a greeting card with this quotation on the inside cover. I have treasured and kept the card available to review when I need inspiration. Over the past thirty-plus years I have had the quotation framed, giving it as a gift for the desks of friends and clients.

Any true story rarely has the same kind of ending that you would expect from a Hollywood movie. That is certainly true of my story. I wish it were as easy as cueing the sunset, leaving with an emotional high, and running the credits. The truth is there is much to be done. The story is not over. Not with me, and possibly not with you either.

The power of one degree saved my life one person, one risk, one gift of hope at a time. And as you have learned, it's my life goal to do whatever I can to multiply that hope and help for as many people as I can. To that end, I'm still working with Dan Merrell at Propeller and cultivating more leads than I chose to share in this book. I wanted you, dear reader, to get a sense of the scope and momentum of this movement. Despite all of my personal challenges and the roadblocks I've hit in my effort to establish One Degree, I am resolved to see it happen to my last breath.

I encourage to you to become involved in the One Degree movement by visiting our website, www.1degree.org. There you'll find specific ways that you can either give or receive hope and help. This is not about donations. In fact, we don't even ask for them. This is about winning the hearts of people and stirring them to see the bigger picture. It is most likely that you are one degree removed from someone who needs hope desperately to face and overcome their challenges. To some degree, great or small, you could be that very person yourself. As I said in the very beginning, one degree is *for* you and it is *by* you. Join me in seeing your own world differently, for sunshine and light always come to those who sincerely hope their dreams will come true.

With hope and help,
PAUL WITTWER

About the Authors

PAUL WITTWER is the founder and owner of Hogtrails, LLC, a mergers and acquisitions consulting company. He has been a millionaire and bankrupt, morbidly obese and physically fit, near the brink of death and full of life, and he's found personal healing and management for physical and emotional challenges like diabetes, coronary disease, homelessness, Post-Traumatic Stress Disorder and obsessive-compulsive disorders. His life is an extraordinary example of hope and possibility. He lives in Nashville, TN.

BRYAN NORMAN is an acquisitions editor for the Nashville-based Christian publishing company, Thomas Nelson Publishers. He joined the company in 2004 after receiving his MA in English Literature and Language at the University of Colorado (Boulder) where he graduated with honors. He has worked with multiple best-selling authors, such as John Eldredge, Donald Miller, Marcus Buckingham, John Maxwell, and more. He lives in Nashville with his wife, Suzanne.